SWAG:

How to Choose and Use
Promotional Products
for Marketing Your Business

Heidi Thorne

ISBN: 1496134222
ISBN-13: 978-1496134226

First Edition, 2011
Second Edition, 2014 (Updated 2016)

Thorne Communications LLC, USA
www.ThorneCommunications.com

SWAG:

How to Choose and Use
Promotional Products
for Marketing Your Business

Heidi Thorne

Contents

My "Why"...ix

PROMO WITH PURPOSE 1

   CHAPTER 1: What is SWAG? 3

   CHAPTER 2: The "Promo With Purpose" Way to Buy
   SWAG 5

PITFALLS AND PRACTICAL ADVICE 19

   CHAPTER 3: When It Comes to Promo, Deal with a Pro .21

   CHAPTER 4: 3 Ways Cheap Ones Can Be the Most
   Expensive 24

   CHAPTER 5: Avoiding the Arts and Crafts Trap 26

   CHAPTER 6: Why Retail Products Cannot be Decorated .30

   CHAPTER 7: The Wrong Tool for the Job 32

   CHAPTER 8: Why You Don't Always Need Something
   Different 34

   CHAPTER 9: Corporate Holiday Gifts: Better Late (or
   Early) Than Never..37

   CHAPTER 10: How Non-Profits Can Avoid a Public
   Relations Nightmare When Buying 39

   CHAPTER 11: Promotional Products Or Toys? How to
   Avoid the Problems With Playthings 42

   CHAPTER 12: Promotional Products We'll Be Laughing at
   in 50 Years (Or Less) 45

   CHAPTER 13: Should You Sell Your Branded Giveaways?
  48

   CHAPTER 14: The Number One Promotional Product
   Mistake Restaurants Make 51

CHAPTER 15: Promotional Sports Schedules Pitch Your Brand All Season Long (Sometimes Really Long!)......53

CHAPTER 16: How to Steal a Page from a Pro Football Promotional Product Playbook 55

CHAPTER 17: Promotional Products Strategies: Location, Location, Location 57

EVENTS 61

CHAPTER 18: 5 Ways to Ditch Dreaded Trade Show Promotional Product Thieves.......................................63

CHAPTER 19: 3 Ways to Avoid the *"Can I Have One For My Kid?"* Problem 66

CHAPTER 20: The Promo Is Right: Attract Trade Show Attendees by Making Your Booth a Game Show........68

CHAPTER 21: 3 Exit Strategies to Green Your Trade Show 70

CHAPTER 22: Why You Need TSA Friendly Promotional Products for Trade Shows 72

GREEN 75

CHAPTER 23: Eco Friendly Definitions 77

CHAPTER 24: Eco Friendly Promotional Product Shopping Guidelines (or Buy This, Not That) 81

CHAPTER 25: 4 Greener Promotional Product Decorating Options 84

CHAPTER 26: Do Fair Trade Promotional Products Exist? 86

CHAPTER 27: How to Green Up Promotional T-Shirt Buying with Life Cycle Assessment 88

CHAPTER 28: When Eco Friendly Promotional Products Don't Work 92

CHAPTER 29: Yuck! A Dark Side of Going Green at Events 94

CHAPTER 30: How Green Are Promotional Products Now? 96

SWAG ORDERING HOW-TO ADVICE 99

CHAPTER 31: Understanding the Buying Process..........101

CHAPTER 32: To Logo or Not to Logo? 104

CHAPTER 33: Tips for Hiring a Graphic Designer for Your Logo 107

CHAPTER 34: What is "Good Artwork" for Imprinting? 110

CHAPTER 35: How to Deal With Itsy Bitsy Imprints......113

CHAPTER 36: How to Imprint QR Codes......................116

CHAPTER 37: 7 Things You Need to Know When Ordering Imprinted T-Shirts 119

CHAPTER 38: What Does T-Shirt Ounce Weight Mean and Why Is It Important? 122

CHAPTER 39: 10 Things You Need to Know When Ordering Embroidered Apparel..................................124

CHAPTER 40: 4 Tips for Handling Rush Promotional Product Orders 128

CHAPTER 41: Do Promotional Products Have a Shelf Life? 130

About Heidi Thorne 132

My "Why"

In well over two decades of being in sales, marketing, advertising and public relations, I've seen micro to mid-sized businesses wrestle with promotional product buying. The available literature just didn't show anyone how to buy this stuff. Most books, seminars, and online resources talked about "marketing," droning on about marketing and business plans. Other resources showcased the obvious mega brands. That has about as much relevance to a one-person entrepreneurship as a book on theoretical physics does to a kid in kindergarten. Typically, promotional product buying was buried in a chapter somewhere, never discussed in depth (if at all), and usually showed a promotion that would cost more than the smaller company would make in years.

Other resources (particularly marketing advice on the web) sniffed at promotional products as if they were the scum of the advertising and marketing world.

Then there were the "practical" books and seminars on "marketing success." The hackneyed ideas I saw in those books were absolutely laughable (not to mention costly for either product or postage). Think sending shoes to "get my foot in the door at your company." Dear Lord!

I saw an information gap. I hope I have filled it in the pages that follow. And I hope that you and your marketing efforts are more successful because of it.

Heidi Thorne

PROMO WITH PURPOSE

CHAPTER 1:
What is SWAG?

What does the term "swag" mean? Actually, it's an acronym for…

Stuff We All Get
Souvenirs, Wearables And Gifts
Souvenirs, Wearables, Awards, Gifts
Souvenirs, Wearables And Giveaways
Sealed With A Gift

Swag can also be referred to as…

Promotional Products
Advertising Specialties
Chotchkies or Tchotchkies

But however you define it, the term "swag" refers to any product that has a logo, message, tagline or some form of personalization on it, usually with the intent of advertising a business, event, association, team, person or cause.

Promotional products have one important attribute that trumps all other forms of advertising: staying power. Some promotional products are retained by recipients for decades. In fact, I have a letter opener that I received from a client in 1998. Better yet, I think about that client whenever I use it.

Swag is generally easy to buy. And it's easy to make mistakes when buying. Those mistakes can be costly, not just in terms of dollars, but in terms of your image and brand.

So what we'll be discussing here is how to buy it right! We'll first discuss the Promo With Purpose way to choose promotional products. Then we'll review some of the pitfalls of promotional products and how to avoid them, special issues relating to events and tradeshows, as well as green buying strategies. Lastly, we'll wrap it up with a how-to advice for purchasing swag.

But it all begins with purpose...

CHAPTER 2:
The "Promo With Purpose" Way to Buy SWAG

Why do you even want to use promotional products anyway? I'll bet if I asked people to honestly answer this question, I'd responses like these:

"Because we've always used 'em."
"Aren't they expecting to get stuff from us?"
"I want one of these for myself."
"We want them to remember us."

First three answers? Not legit reasons for buying. Last answer? Valid, but doesn't go far enough.

Over the years of being a promotional products marketing consultant, I realized that many people had no clue why they were buying these promos. So that's why I developed the "Promo With Purpose" concept to give marketers and business owners the thought roadmap to selecting the right promotion for the purpose at hand.

What the Promo With Purpose concept does is answer the who, what, why, where, when and how for promotional products buying. Be aware that all of the following factors can change over time for both you and your customers. So revisiting the process can be helpful at critical junctures, or even annually, to make sure your promotions are continuing to be effective.

The most important of them is why.

WHY

Before you buy any promotional product, you must begin with what purpose you want that product to serve. Your purpose could be any of the following:

- *To make our logo and organization name visible on the tradeshow floor.*
- *To incentivize people to join to our program or buy from us.*
- *To thank customers for their business.*
- *To educate the public on an important issue.*
- *To get my name visible in the community so they will vote for me.*
- *To get the word out about our upcoming event.*

Notice how each of these statements begins with the word "to." So to begin the thought process for your next purchase, complete this statement:

"I want to use promotional products to_____."

This is your why.

WHO

There are actually two "whos" that you need to consider when buying promotional products: Who you are and who your recipients are. Why is this important?

Let's start with who you are. Be completely honest and answer with who you are, not who you wish you were.

- ***What type of organization are you?*** Are you a company, association, non-profit, entertainer, event planner, tradeshow producer, entrepreneur, team, political party or candidate, municipality, government agency, hospital, college, etc.? This is probably the easiest of the questions.
- ***What word or words would people use to describe your organization?*** Are you friendly, caring, innovative, creative, fun, tech-savvy, tough, or efficient? I'm betting that many of you have never thought about this question.
- ***What are your values?*** Do you value security, freedom, love, learning, power, health, adventure, creativity, etc.?
- ***Who are your organization's members?*** This may encompass many different groups. List all the major ones. What type of people are they? Hardworking, talented, creative, etc.?
- ***Who are the key decision makers in a promotional products purchase?*** I have found that this is often a key determinant of what gets purchased.

When done, complete these statements:
- *"My organization is a(n)_____."*
- *"The word(s) people would use to describe my organization is (are)_____."*
- *"My organization values_____."*

- *"The people in my organization are_____."*
- *"The key decision makers in promotional products purchases are_____."*

Then let's talk about who your audience is.

- **Do you serve a business-to-business (B2B) or business-to-consumer (B2C) market?**
- **What type of organizations make up your market?** Are they companies, associations, non-profits, government agencies, healthcare providers, families, teenagers and young adults, seniors, athletes, students, colleges, etc.?
- **Who are the key decision makers who choose what to buy and who to buy it from?** As illogical as it sounds, sometimes this may be difficult to assess. In B2B markets, I've worked in markets where my customers ranged from administrative assistants all the way up to company ownership. In B2C markets, it can be just as sticky! For instance, in families, the person who decides to spend the money may not be the person who decides what is actually purchased.
- **What word or words would you use to describe your market?** Impatient, happy, adventurous, status quo, nitpicky, hard working, cheap, elegant, fun, etc.?
- **What work or activities does your market do for a living?** Plumbing, daycare, go to school, insurance, family care, sports, leisure, etc.?
- **What environments do your customers spend most of their days?** Are they in their cars, at

home, in an office, on a factory floor, etc.? For some markets, it may be more important to know where your customers spend their leisure time. Is it traveling, on a golf course, in their gardens, at playgrounds, etc.?

- **What are your market's values?** Granted it changes from customer to customer. But you're going to look for any values that seem to be common to the majority of them. Consider the same values that you would for your own organization: security, freedom, love, learning, adventure, health, power, etc.? This is not something you typically discuss with them. You'll have to watch behaviors to assess.

- **What hobbies or leisure activities do they pursue?** Important for both B2B and B2C. Do they golf, travel, go to the movies, go to nightclubs or bars, enjoy spending time with children or pets, etc.? Again, this changes from person to person. But you may know of some common interests that seem to be important to many of them.

What all these questions help determine is what are the triggers that encourage your customers to buy and to buy from you. When done, complete these statements:

- *"My relationship with my customers is (B2B or B2C)_____."*
- *"My customers' organizations are (companies, families, etc.)_____."*
- *"The key decision makers in my customers' organizations (or lives) are_____."*

- *"The word(s) I would use to describe my customer base is (are)_____."*
- *"My customers are (occupation)_____."*
- *"My customers spend most of their days in/at_____. My customers spend their leisure time in/at_____."*
- *"My customers' values are_____."*
- *"My customers' hobbies and interests are_____."*

WHERE

As with the "who" question, there are two "wheres" when considering a promotional product purchase: where you are going to be distributing the item and where your customers are going to be using it. Knowing where you'll be distributing the item can help determine how large, heavy, or portable it needs to be for both yourself and your promotion recipients. Knowing where your customers will typically be using the item can determine what items will be the best fit. For example, you wouldn't want to give refrigerator/file magnets to those who are spending the majority of the time in a vehicle.

Your distribution "where" might also be through the mail or other delivery service. Weight and size are even bigger factors in this case!

As well, think of where your customers would likely be when they are in a buying mood for what you sell. You want your promotion there! Drill down to the room and personal location. Are they at a desk? In the kitchen? It's why Yellow Pages phone directories worked for as long as they did before the Internet became the norm. People were going there to find and dial up solutions to their immediate needs.

- *"I will be distributing my promotion at/through_____."*
- *"My customers will likely use my promotion at_____."*
- *"My customers typically will make a buying decision for my product at_____."*

WHEN

Very closely related to "where" is "when." If your "when" is coming up next week, that will severely limit your choices of promotional items. And knowing when your customers are in a buying mood can help determine a place where you might want to put your promotion. What is happening at that moment when a buying decision process begins?

- *"I will be distributing my promotion on (date)_____ which is _____ days away from now."*
- *"My customers are in a buying mood when_____."*

HOW

The effectiveness of your promotion, as well as whether you stay on budget or not, is often determined by how you distribute it.

Will it be through direct mail? Response (not actual sales!) rates for direct mail can be as low as 1-2%. So you'll have to buy a lot more of whatever you're distributing to get an acceptable return.

If you're distributing it at a tradeshow, indiscriminately giving out your promotion to everyone who wanders by your booth is a recipe for budget blunders. Qualifying booth visitors, and only giving your promotions to those that do, can save you money on promotional products as well as on time and effort wasted on non-qualifying leads.

Also knowing how your customers will be using your promotion can help you decide what investment you wish to make. For example, if you are using branded disposable drinkware at an event, you don't want to invest too much into something that will be trashed or recycled as soon as the event is over.

- *"I plan to distribute my promotion by _____."*
- *"My customers will be using my promotion for _____."*

WHAT

This is where is all comes together. Your analysis of all the above pieces will help you determine what to buy.

Two final "what" questions are needed prior to the final analysis: What is your budget? What quantity will you need? It is easy to determine if it is a mailing and you have the list quantity available or for events where each attendee will receive an item. For tradeshows, you do not have to buy enough product to distribute to each attendee unless you have an arrangement to put your promotion in attendee welcome bags. Planning for 10-20% of total attendance to stop by your booth is usually more than enough, especially if you are going to be carefully distributing to only qualified prospects.

- *"My budget for this particular promotion is_____."*
- *"The quantity of promotion pieces needed is_____."*
- *(For events and tradeshows) "The anticipated total number of attendees is_____."*
- *(For tradeshows) "I anticipate _____ visitors to our booth."*

PUTTING IT ALL TOGETHER (A REAL LIFE SCENARIO)

To illustrate the Promo With Purpose concept in action, let's look at a likely scenario for many of the clients I serve. I work with wholesalers who sell equipment and supplies to residential home services contractors. So let's see how they might answer the Promo With Purpose questions.

WHY

- *"I want to use promotional products to keep my store location info handy for contractors while they're on the job."*

WHO

Organization:

- *"My organization is a distributor for brand name equipment and supplies with four locations."*

- *"The words people would use to describe my organization are <u>friendly, willing to go the extra mile, expensive.</u>"*
- *"My organization values <u>friendship and caring.</u>"*
- *"The people in my organization are <u>fun and friendly.</u>"*
- *"The key decision makers in promotional products purchases are <u>my purchasing agent and me.</u>"*

Customers:
- *"My relationship with my customers is <u>B2B.</u>"*
- *"My customers' organizations are <u>contractors in the trades.</u>"*
- *"The key decision makers in my customers' organizations are <u>typically the business owner or foreman.</u>"*
- *"The words I would use to describe my customer base are <u>busy, distracted, impatient, hard working, no nonsense, price conscious.</u>"*
- *"My customers are <u>contractors who may be either a one-person shop or a have a few trucks and techs.</u>"*
- *"My customers spend most of their days in <u>their vehicles. Some office time, but may work from home. My customers spend their leisure time at home with family, golf course, and sports activities (primarily with kids).</u>"*
- *"My customers' values are <u>freedom and independence</u>"*

- *"My customers' hobbies and interests are spending time with family, golfing, sports events, travel, motorsports and auto collecting."*

WHERE

- *"I will be distributing my promotion at <u>an annual industry tradeshow.</u>"*
- *"My customers will likely use my promotion at <u>the office or in their vehicles.</u>"*
- *"My customers typically will make a buying decision for my product at <u>the office. However, for parts or equipment unexpectedly needed while on the job, they may make a decision at the jobsite or on the road.</u>"*

WHEN

- *"I will be distributing my promotion on <u>March 30 which is 30 days away from now.</u>"*
- *"My customers are in a buying mood when <u>they are trying to complete a job and need supplies or equipment fast. They also plan on bigger inventory buys in the pre-season.</u>"*

HOW

- *"I plan to distribute my promotion by <u>giving them to show visitors who stop by our booth and talk with us.</u>"*
- *"My customers will be using my promotion for <u>handy reference.</u>"*

WHAT

- *"My budget for this particular promotion is $1,000."*
- *(For events and tradeshows) "The anticipated total number of attendees is 2,500."*
- *(For tradeshows, 10-20% of total attendance) "I anticipate 250-500 visitors to our booth."*

ANALYSIS

This B2B organization serves a harried, no fluff, highly mobile crowd that just wants to get the job done. And with freedom and independence as big values, their customers are not interested in being told what to do either. So the wholesaler should choose promotions that send a message of *"we're here when you need us and we'll help you get the job done!"* Choosing an item that can be used in a vehicle would be good to build parts and rush order business. Items that could be used in the office might also work for promoting pre-season inventory buys.

Notice that there's a disconnect between the values of the organization and its customers. The organization thrives on being a friendly, albeit more expensive, service-oriented go-to source. Yet their customers are more cut-to-the-chase and price conscious. The organization must emphasize their convenience and competence to appeal to this crowd.

Off the job, sports are a big deal for their customers whether it's watching, playing, or supporting their kids. So sports themed items could be a good choice. With the show being in the early spring, anything to do with baseball, golf, basketball (pro playoffs), or hockey (also playoffs) might be options. However, for greatest longevity, baseball and golf would be most viable since those seasons run well into the fall.

The show at which they plan to distribute this promotion is about a month away. That is usually good timing for a buy like this and eliminates rush charges. Their budget of $1,000 should be adequate for a buy of 250-500 items. That would put each item in the $2-$4 price range.

What might this organization consider? Of course, choices will depend on what's available at that point in time. But as of this writing, these items could be:

- *Magnetic/adhesive sports schedules for use in the office which indicate all of the organization's locations and product brands or types offered.*
- *Mobile convenience gadgets such as holders for office supplies or cell phones which feature hotline numbers and location info.*
- *Notepads that fit in a shirt pocket which have location and phone information. Surprisingly, with a highly mobile market like this, notepads and pens are still hot because it's usually faster to jot down a note than fumble with a small or virtual on-screen mobile phone keyboard.*
- *Sticky adhesive notes that can be used in the office or vehicle.*
- *Travel mugs.*
- *Water bottles.*
- *Clipboards for easy writing while in a vehicle.*

- *Large, letter-size planner pads, possibly with a grid for sketching ideas or layouts.*
- *Laminated line cards listing all available products and brands, locations, and possibly other handy reference material. A client of mine does this with their information on the front and a metric conversion chart on the back. A hanging hole is provided for use in the office. But it is an easy item to stash into a folder, too. Can also be made with magnets for hanging on file cabinets.*

Next we'll talk about some specific issues relating to swag that can either make or break the effectiveness of your promotion.

PITFALLS AND PRACTICAL ADVICE

CHAPTER 3:
When It Comes to Promo,
Deal with a Pro

In my networking, I've run across many printers who also offer promotional products in addition to the printing of brochures, flyers, and direct mail. Same can be said for marketing consultants, ad agencies, and graphic designers. Doesn't bother me one bit. I think there's enough business for everyone. Plus, these folks can be great power partners for someone like me. So if a customer is very comfortable working with any of them for these items, he should continue to do so.

One word of caution: Some of these providers are not promotional products experts and usually sell these items as add-on sales to their other business. What does these mean for you? In many cases, it means that they may not have the relationships or experience to adequately advise you or may have limited selection.

Sourcing promotional products is more than just looking up an item in a database. I've run into several allied marketing partners who wail about the poor quality of items they found in the databases (not all promo products are created equal). Or they complain about how much time and effort it takes to sift through the databases to find exactly what they're looking for. Problem is they're busy and don't have the time to develop relationships with key vendors, review samples, go to tradeshows and training, etc. to become skilled advisors in this arena. One promotional industry database alone has over 750,000 products listed—yes, three-quarters of a million. So you do need to know your way around the industry to use these database tools properly.

Remember, these folks are in business to sell the products or services for which they are experts. So don't expect them to have all the answers about swag. If you are working with a marketing consultant, graphic designer, or advertising agency, ask them if they have promotional products vendor recommendations for you.

Another word of caution: If you enter discussions about buying swag with these types of advisors, ask to have their recommended promotional products vendor in the discussions from the start. I cannot tell you how many times I've been approached by a graphic designer or marketing consultant to source a product that does not exist or to imprint a design that is impossible or outrageously expensive. They inevitably set up their clients for disappointment. And once the client has the fantasy promo stuck in his head, it's hard to refocus, usually resulting in the client scrapping the idea altogether. Having a swag expert on your team right from the start avoids wasted time and effort chasing an unattainable vision.

Another case of this problem is the big box office supply retailers. They do caboodles of promo business both in stores and online. Are the associates/workers who man the copy and print center going to be great promotional products marketing advisors for you? Probably not. However, they will usually make sure that all the orders are completed according to their procedures.

I think the reason that the office suppliers have made such a strong showing in the promo arena is that they are appealing to new entrepreneurs. Newbies haven't built up their network of advisors, but they do need office supplies from the beginning. So the office supply just happens to be the closest thing they have to promotional products marketing consulting. Probably okay early on, but new entrepreneurs will need to expand their advisor horizons as they grow.

The strength of all these non-specialized promotional products sellers is also testament to how poorly many swag distributors market themselves. If you are evaluating working with a number of distributors, watch how they promote their businesses. If they don't use promotional products themselves, why would you want to buy from them? Apart from swag, how do they market their business? Not impressed? Then walk away.

Bottom line, deal with a pro when it comes to promo.

CHAPTER 4:
3 Ways Cheap Ones Can Be the Most Expensive

"Imprinted pens as low as $0.19 each," says the ad. Wow! At that price you could stock up and promote your business on a shoestring. But you may end up paying more, lots more, in the long run for this promotional product buy. Here's how...

The Asterisk (*). Ads for imprinted marketing products that tout super low prices may have an * somewhere near the pricing information. When you then flip over to the ordering page, you'll see a host of fees that can easily double a product's price when all is said and done. In reality, there is no getting around costs such as set-up fees, taxes, shipping and handling. They are necessary expenses that must be passed on to you in order for the vendor to remain in business.

Set-up fees are the costs for the vendor to set up equipment to imprint your giveaways. When you see an ad that says "no set-up fees," those fees are built into the price. You will be paying them one way or another.

Shipping is the actual freight incurred to deliver your order from the factory to your door. In most cases the factory is not in the same location as your distributor. So your order may be coming from across the country instead of across town. Handling can include time and paperwork needed to process your order, estimating, production monitoring, and other costs not accounted for elsewhere.

Another way the asterisk can mean more money is with the phrase "as low as..." Often products are advertised with the price you would pay if you bought boatloads of them, say 10,000 or more.

Give Today, Trash Tomorrow. A client purchased some cheap imprinted pens from a low-cost provider that "exploded" on impact. Yep, the ink cartridge flew right out of the barrel if you pressed too hard when writing. In addition to some safety issues, flimsy imprinted items do not offer you longevity which is one of the greatest benefits of promotional products.

When You Care Enough to Give the Very Least. What do you think you're telling your customers and prospects by giving them cheap promotional products? First, it tells them that you may not be able to afford anything better. In the back of their minds they might be thinking, *"Hmm, maybe they're not that successful. What's wrong with them?"* Next, it tells them that you want their business so much, you're spending a pittance on an item that'll be trashed tomorrow. The underlying mental note, *"If they're cutting corners here, will they be cutting corners on service too?"*

Swag is an investment. Treat is as such.

CHAPTER 5:
Avoiding the Arts and Crafts Trap

I am so lucky to work with some very creative clients and graphic designers. They come up with some incredible ideas for promotional products. Always helps me stretch in terms of sourcing and finding solutions. However, their creativity can sometimes lead to unproductive and profit-stealing ideas.

Here's what sometimes happens. They have an inspiration for a giveaway that is a perfect tie-in with a theme or company image. They propose the idea to their bosses or clients and get buy-in. That's when they call me as a promotional products distributor. Unfortunately, the products they often envision don't exist. Let the sourcing circus begin!

At that point, I usually have to do an extensive database search to find something close. But whatever I find just doesn't quite meet their artistic visions. The search continues. After coming up short, they now have to go back to their companies or clients and offer something completely different. More time wasted and potentially unhappy clients and bosses. And I feel awful for not being able to turn someone's dream into reality.

Let's look at a few examples to illustrate…

I've had requests for custom figurines and models from several people over the years. Very, very cool idea! And it's an idea that would have tremendous impact. Are custom figures and models possible? Sure. However, unless you are a very large corporation, the investment in design and mold fees make this idea unworkable. I usually get requests like this from organizations that need maybe 50-500 of the items to use for their very best clients and prospects. For this type of item to make sense, you usually need to be looking at a quantity of 10,000 to 100,000 or more. Plus, if the item even has the possibility of being considered a toy, it now must pass safety inspections (particularly for lead and choking hazards) which can run into the hundreds. On top of this, add the time it takes for custom manufacturing, often overseas. Try months.

Reaching a dead end for the custom figures, the client or designer sometimes looks to buying a similar item from retail and doctoring it up as a promotional product. Custom handmade labels, paint, strings, bows, glue, cellophane wrap…it becomes an arts and crafts project. Plus, there usually is a scramble to find the necessary quantity in retail. A treasure hunt of local stores ensues.

Need to see this in action? Take a look at some winning self-promotion campaigns in the graphic design magazines. Arts and crafts extravaganzas! (I have seen these manifestations in real life, too.) Imagine how many hours and dollars are poured into these projects that could have been spent more productively, such as in networking or other sales producing activities. Even worse is that if they're using these promotions for themselves, chances are they are suggesting similar, time and money consuming ideas for their clients.

Sometimes it's not the item that's the problem. It's the decoration. Most common problem is with T-shirts. *"Wow, wouldn't it be cool if we could have the imprint running around the neckline, along the shoulder, down the sleeve, and then from the front to the back?"* Cool? Yes. However, some of these "cool" decorating schemes require special handling and may not even be possible on standard decorating equipment. As well, some ideas would require decorating prior to construction. Again, only a huge quantity might make this viable.

So how can you avoid the arts and crafts trap in buying promotional products?

Get Your Promotional Products Distributor Involved Early. Your promotional products distributor can be a great friend. Partner up with a distributor who is marketing oriented. Let him know what you're thinking about before offering an idea to your staff, boss or client. This will avoid disappointment for all and save time in getting to a viable solution.

Understand the Limitations of Imprinting. Your distributor can provide you with the imprinting specs (area available, locations, etc.) for promotional items of interest. He can provide guidance and information on available imprinting processes so you can choose what's best for the project and the product.

Realize that Time is Money. Every minute you spend crafting a whiz-bang, one-off type promotion is one minute you need to bill or write off. Clients and bosses are paying you to be a marketing or design expert, not a piecework worker. And if you outsource the crafting, the cost of the promotion can increase dramatically. So whether it's your time or someone else's, labor costs need to be seriously considered for these types of projects.

CHAPTER 6:
Why Retail Products
Cannot be Decorated

Usually get this type of request as we near the holidays: *"I would like to give out (fill in latest super gadget name here) to my clients for Christmas."* And, usually, I have to tell them no or the item is very expensive to purchase as a decorated promotional product. Then the response is, *"But I can get them at Wal-Mart for $4. Why can't I get them from you for that price? I'm buying 15 of them."*

Before I get my dander up, I have to remember that to someone who's not in the business of providing these products, the prospect of not being able to do this seems insane. Don't think I don't sympathize.

So some explanation would be in order...

Retail Buys in Bulk. You may think that your quantity of 25 pieces might be huge, especially if it's an expensive item. But that quantity is minuscule compared to the 25 truckloads that retail outlets might buy. When you buy a product as a promotional product, it is a separate small batch order that has to be hand-picked and processed. Thus the higher price.

Manufacturers Protect Their Brands. Makers of brand name merchandise fiercely protect their names, logos, and reputations. Think of how disastrous it would be if a competitor or unethical company put their name on your product! How would you react? A manufacturer can sue you for putting your logo on a product that they have not authorized for promotional use. When a brand name product is made available for promotional use, the wholesaler has paid for the brand licensing rights—which also adds to the cost of the product.

Retail Products May Not Withstand Imprinting Processes. My favorite example is one my client gave me. One of their former suppliers had purchased some vinyl businesses folios in retail and then imprinted using a hot stamp process. The vinyl is puckered from the heat and the imprint can almost be rubbed off because the ink could not properly adhere to the surface. I keep this real life "show and tell" to illustrate why not to dabble in retail for promotional products.

Your Brand is at Stake (and So is Your Money). What if the retail-cum-promotional-product turns out very badly if imprinted? Is that a good selling tool for you? You will look like you are competing on Amateur Hour. You look too cheap to do it right, too sloppy to pay attention to details, and too unprofessional to hire. Alternatively, if your imprinted retail product is too bad to use and has to be trashed, you've wasted your money. You don't even want to donate it because it has your name on it and you don't want that falling into potential customers' hands.

CHAPTER 7:
The Wrong Tool for the Job

"They'll think that's useless," my client scoffed as I showed him an imprintable multi-tool in his target price range for his contractor clients. *"These guys want brand name stuff. My dad would probably use that to just clip his nails."*

And he was absolutely correct.

If you work with anyone in the trades, as many of my clients do, you become very aware that the wrench-turners are pretty attached to their wrenches...and anything else in their tool boxes. So giving them promotional tools that are less than professional grade is a waste of money. You'd be better off giving them fast food or gas gift certificates which they would use.

What my client understood is that you need to get inside the head of your target audience when selecting appropriate promotional products. You need to understand what's important to them.

When you distribute a promotion that's sub-par for your audience, you also appear to be a poser or "not one of us." This is not only relevant for the trades, but for any audience where membership (whether or official or unofficial) is based on proving oneself worthy to be a part of the club. Think skateboarders, garden clubs, online video game communities or biker gangs.

The problem is that the really good stuff, such as the pro grade tools my client referred to, are really expensive, too. Additionally, as we discussed previously, brand name retail products present a host of issues in terms of brand infringement and difficulties with imprintability.

So what should you do when the market is tough, getting appropriate items is rough, and your budget is not enough?

Dig Deeper. During your Promo With Purpose analysis, you discovered more about your market's values and extracurricular activities. If you can't find something appropriate for an obvious tie-in, go for a secondary value or interest. They may be less sensitive in that area, offering you more options.

Help Them Do Their Jobs Cheaper, Better, Faster. I wasn't really joking earlier when I suggested giving tradespeople fast food restaurant or gas gift certificates. They're in their vehicles a lot! So being able to swing through a drive-thru to get a free cup of coffee on the way to the next job or to fill up the gas tank for free is a much appreciated gift. Think of different kinds of promotional "tools" that you can use to help your customers be the success they want to be. You're more likely to be regarded as a partner in their business. And isn't that what you really want anyway?

CHAPTER 8:
Why You Don't Always Need
Something Different

With some clients I get the same litany every year when we're working on their promotional product buys: *"I'm looking for something different."* I always have to ask, *"What do you mean by different?"* To that I usually get an *"I don't know"* or a blank stare.

Here are some interpretations of something different. In thinking about your own purchases and need for novelty, do any of these ring true for you?

Different Than Last Year. The client has become bored with what he distributed last year and is looking for something new.

The Newest, Latest, and Greatest. These clients want whatever is hot this year, no matter what it is and regardless of if it is right for their company.

Same Thing With a Twist. Let's say they've been giving away pens for years. These clients want a pen again, but a different design or color.

Something Cheaper. Some clients think that if they choose something different than before, they will save money. Sometimes that is true, but not always. They often don't know how to tell me that they are budget-strapped. So this saves face.

Unique, Way-Out, One-of-a-Kind. These clients want to stand out from the crowd no matter what. They want to be seen as innovators and market leaders. They want highly customized items that one could not purchase anywhere.

Whatever category you fall into, here are some things to keep in mind if you are thinking about switching to new types of promotional products:

Customers Don't Get Bored Quickly. You may have seen your same notepad or pen a thousand times and you are bored with it. Your clients, on the other hand, appreciate your generosity even if it is the same thing that they have received before. I have had clients who have ordered essentially the same items for nearly a decade. Their customers have used up what was given the previous year and like to get replacements.

The Latest Hot Item May Not Be Hot for Your Company. Recently reusable shopping bags have been all the rage. But if you have a business-to-business clientele, it may not be an optimal choice.

Don't Change for Sake of Change. Even if you use the same item such as a pen, if you keep changing the design or color, you will likely have a hodgepodge inventory of promotional items. This jumbles your image building efforts. It also may show that you are not that successful and trying to squeeze every last dime out of your marketing budget by using up your on-hand inventory, even if it doesn't present a unified image.

Cheaper Is Not Always Better. Granted, there may be times where you do have to cut back on expenses. But don't sacrifice your marketing image just to save a few bucks. Cheaper items which may not be of the same quality as you were using before can hurt your reputation.

Highly Customized Equals High Price. Always have to chuckle when I encounter clients who want to have some way out custom product and then want some ridiculously low quantity such as 25. Yes, a truly custom product that makes you stand out from the crowd is an image builder. However, it is a costly strategy since custom products require additional costs such as mold fees and high quantities (maybe into the tens of thousands). Carefully consider whether this is a custom item you would like to use over time. If it is, then the investment in customization may be worth it.

Way Out Unique Products May Have Limited Use. It may be attention getting, but if it has low utility, a way out unique product decreases the long advertising impact that promotional products typically provide.

CHAPTER 9:
Corporate Holiday Gifts: Better Late (or Early) Than Never

Oh darn! You got so busy around the holidays that you didn't have time to send out gifts to your clients, you know, those folks that keep you in business. Oh well, guess they'll have to wait until next year. Actually, if you do wait 'til it does become "next year," you might just score big with your clients. Here's a story to illustrate.

One of my best friends in the graphic design biz told me about a client holiday gift nightmare that turned into a delightful surprise for everyone. His company had ordered gifts and there was a problem with getting the order done in time for Christmas. Of course, his company's initial reaction was frustration and disappointment since clients would receive their gifts in January, well after New Year's. Luckily, all that melted away when the nice comments from recipients started coming in. Because the gifts were received after the flood of other greetings and gifts, it got a lot more attention and appreciation.

So if you missed sending gifts for Hanukkah or Christmas, why not consider a New Year's surprise?

On the opposite side of the gift giving spectrum, you might also want to consider giving holiday gifts early, like before Thanksgiving. I traditionally give my advertising clients their gifts just before or during the week of Thanksgiving. They'll be able to share the goodies with family while celebrating Turkey Day or while decorating for the holidays that weekend.

Timing can be an important part of your promotional gift giving strategy. But always remember to show your appreciation...better late (or early) than never.

CHAPTER 10:
How Non-Profits Can Avoid a Public Relations Nightmare When Buying

Let's say you're launching a fund raising campaign for a children's welfare organization. You've decided to distribute an imprinted T-shirt as a thank you gift for donations. Great idea that could help spread the word about your work as the shirts are worn in the community. So you find an attractively price T-shirt online. Prices like that will help you save funds for your cause. But wait! That inexpensive price may turn into an expensive public relations nightmare. Here's how...

You might be thinking that because it is cheaper, the problem may be that it is poorly constructed or uses lower grade materials. Yes, that might be possible. But more importantly, the shirt's material or construction could have been produced in an environment or in a country that allows child labor. In the 2009 U.S. Department of Labor's List of Goods Produced by Child or Forced Labor, a dozen or so countries were reported as having incidences of child labor for cotton production and three were noted for garment manufacture. These are serious fair trade issues that are beginning to take center stage in the world marketplace.

Imagine the backlash in the press, on Twitter, and in blogs that would result from you, as a children's support organization, using a promotional product suspected to be made by child labor. Ouch! Your campaign will quickly go from fund raising to defense which will eat up much needed funds for your mission.

In a similar scenario, organizations that support green efforts would be well advised to look at how green their imprinted giveaways are. Groups that support American workers should also be careful. Many flag-waving promotional items are made outside the United States' borders. You get the picture. Whatever item you choose to market your organization must be made with materials and labor that mirror your values. Even if you are not with the organization itself, but are just a sponsor, you will be doing yourself and the group you support a big favor by selecting giveaways that are aligned with the cause.

Think these are fictional "what if" scenarios? They're not. I've actually seen incidences where some U.S. unions (they're not my clients...yet!) used "Made in (Insert non-U.S.A. Country Here)" promotional products for mass distribution to the public. Ouch again!

What can help you avoid this public relations nightmare?

Clarify Your Mission, Message, and Values. Be very specific about what you are trying to accomplish and what is important to your organization. Relay that mission to your swag distributor so she knows what to avoid or recommend.

Determine What is Unacceptable. Knowing the message you are trying to communicate, determine what aspects of a product would be contrary to that. Supporting children's welfare? No child labor. Starting an eco-friendly campaign? No petroleum-based plastic products. Celebrating a national and patriotic holiday? No overseas manufactured products.

If in Doubt, Ask. If you cannot readily determine the fair trade or eco-friendly status of a promotional product, ask your distributor. If he cannot provide you with adequate documentation or certification (such as for fair trade or organic status), it would be recommended to continue looking. Similarly, he should be able to provide the country of origin for the item in question. Getting a sample can help, too.

CHAPTER 11:
Promotional Products Or Toys? How to Avoid the Problems With Playthings

"Aw, isn't that cute? That will get lots of attention."
Walk the aisles of almost any major promotional product show and you'll see hundreds of cute and clever items—stuffed toys, games, model cars, stress balls, you name it!—that are sure to get "gotta have it" responses from your customers and tradeshow visitors.

The problem with many of these "cute" promotions is that they cross from being promotions to playthings. Many parents take these items home to their children. Aside from the fact that you just wasted your marketing dollars on a six-year old, there are unfortunately some new and significant legal issues that also come into play:

Most Promotional Products are Not Intended to Be Toys. Many of them will have warning labels about not being intended for children under a certain age (often three to six years). With small parts, they can become a choking hazard. Certain paints and materials can present health issues (for example, bisphenol A, or BPA). This enters lawsuit territory and everyone up and down the supply chain—manufacturer, distributors, marketer—

could be party to it. Even people's pets need to be noted in safety warnings in some cases!

New Regulations are Getting Tougher. Recently, consumer protections were instituted that now require items that can be classified as toys to pass safety testing, primarily for lead content, but may also include other testing. Buyers of custom promotional playthings will now be assessed a charge for this testing which can run into the hundreds of dollars. Stock design products have usually been tested prior to them being made available for sale.

This is not intended to scare you away from using playful promotions. Taking some preventive measures will help keep you and your promotions' recipients safe:

Assess Your Audience. If your audience is the general public and there is a possibility that children will receive the items you distribute, plan on using an item that is non-toxic and would be suitable for all ages. If it is primarily older adults, it is not as critical, but should be considered since parents and grandparents are always on the lookout for goodies for their children and grandchildren.

Reject Items that are Not Easily Identified as Toy or Promotion. The one that sticks out in my mind is stress balls. They are often made into colorful characters and shapes. They are not intended to be used by small children or pets since they can shred off and are not subjected to the same testing as genuine toys. Skip this type of item for general public distribution or in situations where it may be likely to be passed on to children.

Include a Safety Warning in Imprint. Though it will not completely protect you in a lawsuit, including a "Not a Toy" or "Not Intended for Small Children or Pets" warning somewhere in your imprint could put recipients on alert about what you are giving them.

Request Safety Compliance Documentation. Your promotional product distributor should be able to provide you with documentation on either the compliance or testing of your item choice if you require it. This would be certainly be necessary for any promotion with far reaching distribution, such as a national franchise chain. If you have a large open-to-the-public event, you may also wish to have this.

CHAPTER 12:
Promotional Products We'll Be
Laughing at in 50 Years (Or Less)

One of my favorite articles in a promotional products industry journal is one that takes a look back at hot items from 10, 20, or even 50 years ago. Absolutely hilarious and oh so reflective of the values, styles, and habits of the day. Some shining examples are all the imprinted smoking paraphernalia, toys that don't have a prayer of passing a child safety test, and all manner of gadgetry that could solve any antiquated desktop dilemma (rotary phone dialers anyone?). Sadly, and inevitably, they have become promotional product dinosaurs, their plastic fossils to live on for centuries in landfills—okay, that's fodder for another discussion on trends, but I digress.

So I thought I would project myself 50 years into the future and take a look back at some of the future dinosaur products that you might want to reconsider buying today. Not only will you make purchasing decisions that will have longer lasting impact, you'll help keep these short-lived items out of the waste stream.

Mousepads. Sure, they're still useful. But as mobile computing continues to grow in market dominance, people are less and less tied to a desktop computer, making mousepads obsolete. And how many mousepads can you use? One at a time. So yours better be outrageously cool to become that one.

Anything Tech. Technology marches forward at a rapid pace, making today's 1-8 gigabyte promotional USB drive incapable of handling the terabyte rich content of tomorrow. It wasn't too many years ago when imprinted CDs were one of the hottest items. Even funnier is to remember promos that were designed around 3.5" floppy disks. I see mobile apps and cloud computing obliterating the need for distributing USB drives in the future. And where will all those drives end up? Take a guess. Think about how your customers are going to use them before you buy. If you distribute your brochure on one, they'll review it, and then wonder what to do with the drive. How many of these drives can you use and carry around?

Promotional USB drives are great because they do eliminate the need for distribution of paper which is an earth-friendly score. More eco-friendly USB drives made of recycled or sustainable materials are also now available. But even then, please use them judiciously and look for ways to direct customers and prospects to your online resources before automatically resorting to a USB drive.

Magnets. Where would the promotional product world be without the ubiquitous fridge magnet? This promotional product staple is already waning because we have less metallic surfaces on which to place them. Cubicles are made of fabric panels. Desks and other furniture are made of composite materials. Plastic surfaces are everywhere. And adhesive-backed alternatives can wreak havoc on some surfaces. So what will replace them? There are new removable adhesive and static cling products that will adhere, without residue, to almost a wide variety of surfaces. Look for new entries in this area.

Those are just three items on their way to the promotional product history books.

So what will still be around in 50 years? I don't see T-shirts going away anytime soon, but even those will have their own evolution into more eco-friendly and socially responsible options.

CHAPTER 13:
Should You Sell Your
Branded Giveaways?

What if you could get paid for marketing your organization by selling your branded promotional products? You would offset some of the cost of your marketing and maybe create a profit center, too. Sweet!

While everyone would like to duplicate the brand extension success of an organization such as Harley-Davidson, creating a branded merchandise "store" is not for everyone. Here are scenarios where this strategy would work best:

Dedicated Customer Base United by Consumption of the Company's Main Products or Services. Biker groups, sci-fi fans, sports teams, and schools are examples. The more rabid the fan or customer base is, the more likely this strategy would be a winner.

Events. Branded promotional merchandise sold in conjunction with a special event has commemorative value. Think about the Olympics and Super Bowl.

Dealer Networks. If your customers are dealers of your products or services, they are often looking for additional ways to promote them to their customers. As well, offering authorized promotional merchandise helps you control the company image throughout the dealer network.

If your business falls into one of these categories, here are some additional considerations before you get started:

Don't Buy Huge Inventories. Until you have a sales track record, do not buy large inventories even if the per piece price is attractive. Even at a low price, unsold items waste marketing funds.

Select a Few Products to Start. Your initial store should only include a few key products to see if you get any response. Usually wearable items such as T-shirts, caps, and tote bags are good initial choices.

Establish a Retail Sales Tax Number. If retail sales tax is collected by your state, you will need to establish a tax identification number if you do not have one already. You will also need to start reporting these revenues and forwarding the collected taxes to your state taxing authority. This is quite a shock to many service providers who typically do not have a retail side of their business. This will add more administrative duties to your company. So carefully consider whether the anticipated revenues are worth the additional administrative costs. Ask your bookkeeping and accounting professionals for assistance.

Designate Someone to Handle Store Activity. If handling retail type sales is not customary for your company, make sure you designate someone to monitor sales activity and order follow-up. This is a function that could easily fall through the cracks. Establishing procedures for handling is an absolute necessity.

Price It Right. Here is where you can easily make a mistake using this strategy. As with any business, you will need to add on an appropriate mark-up so that this venture does not turn into a money loser. Some companies say that because those who buy and use the branded merchandise are advertising for them, they are willing to incur a loss. There is some validity to that. But, as mentioned above, this strategy will require additional administrative effort which is not free to you.

CHAPTER 14:
The Number One Promotional Product Mistake Restaurants Make

You've just enjoyed a delicious meal at the restaurant and your server has brought you the check. Typically the check is in a folder with the restaurant's name on it. Then you open the folder and what do you find? A pen with an imprinted message for any place but the restaurant at which you are currently dining.

As someone who eats out at restaurants about 50 percent of the time due to my workstyle and lifestyle—and because I'm a horrific cook!—I've had ample opportunity to observe this marketing blunder. Here's a sampling of the pens I have encountered while paying for my dining check: hospitals and doctors (Not good tie-ins with restaurants!), local colleges, mechanics (Where was that pen used last?), banks, mortgage companies, churches, generic pens with chewed ends (Eeewww!), child care, and so much more. However, the worst example is the pen from a competing restaurant. Ouch! What a hit to any restaurant's branding.

Plus, when servers use pens for businesses other than the restaurant, the other businesses are getting advertising to the restaurant's customer base for free. Again, ouch!

Why does this happen? Restaurants often don't provide imprinted pens to servers for use by guests because they feel that the servers will swipe the pens for use at home. So they make their servers provide pens for guests. Of course, the servers are not going to invest in promoting the restaurant and use whatever pens they can get their hands on for free from other local businesses.

Or maybe there's a concern about the environment and using too many plastic pens that may just get thrown in the trash. Then a biodegradable pen made from corn would be a great choice. A pen made from an edible crop...sounds like a great tie-in for a restaurant.

Granted, when a restaurant buys imprinted promotional pens it is an expense. But when compared to the marketing damage done through the use of pens that have negative connotations or promote competitors, it is marketing money well spent.

CHAPTER 15:
Promotional Sports Schedules Pitch Your Brand All Season Long (Sometimes Really Long!)

As a diehard football fan, baseball season just never seems to end for me. Heck, I'm already getting antsy for Hall of Fame weekend before even the first pitch of baseball season is thrown. But baseball's looonnnnnnng season means great advertising opportunities for you and your business with promotional baseball schedules. And unlike football which usually has only a couple game days per week, baseball has several games on various days, meaning your promotion could be referred to multiple times per week.

My clients have loved using them over the years, especially with a healthy crosstown rivalry here in Chicago, which brings up a point for cities like Chicago with multiple teams for the same sport. Which team should you promote along with your business? Your favorite or your clients' favorite? Or should you promote both area teams? My initial suggestion would be to promote both on the same schedule (yes, there are schedules that promote both). However, if you're absolutely sure that your client base favors one team over the other, then go with the team that THEY want to see, which may or may not be your favorite. As well, if your business is patronized by fans from one team over the other, go with that team. An example would be restaurants or bars that are near Chicago's Wrigley Field which would make Cubs promotions more appropriate.

Be aware, also, that due to licensing issues, you cannot promote a particular team's name along with your own. On team schedules, you will see teams referred to as a city name along with their National or American League affiliation. For example, the Chicago Cubs would be listed at Chicago (NL) on your schedules.

CHAPTER 16:
How to Steal a Page from a Pro Football Promotional Product Playbook

Watching a recent NFL playoff game, I was certainly struck by commentary that the noise in the Seattle Seahawks stadium from the fans had such a dramatic effect on visiting teams. Who says fans don't get into the game? They're a huge "player!"

And helping to fuel that fervor is the fan gear that brings color and solidarity to sports-loving crowds. Prime example is the Pittsburgh Steelers' "Terrible Towels." Did you realize that they've been using 'em since 1975? It's a promotional product legend! (Google it to find out more.)

Good thing about these kinds of items is that they can become collectibles. So how can you use this strategy for your sports team or even event or tradeshow? Here are couple neat ideas:

Start Your Own Swag Legend. Take a page out of the Steelers' promotional playbook and encourage your fans or customers to take pics of themselves in fantastic locations with your promotional product (with, ahem, some restrictions of course) and post them on social media. Helps to engage them in your promotion.

Make Some Noise! Get megaphones that are designed to also be used as popcorn holders during the game or event. Dual-duty helps cut promotional costs. Saves green, goes green! Other noisemakers would work, too.

CHAPTER 17:
Promotional Products Strategies:
Location, Location, Location

Was having a quick dinner at an iconic Chicago area restaurant chain. Love their Italian beef, hot dogs, salads, pasta, and more. On this particular visit, I was having a salad and got the packaged utensils. In the package was a sample of sugarfree gum. Interesting.

Most restaurants don't sell gum. But many people do like to have gum after a meal. So think about it. The gum manufacturer placed their sample where people will likely use it...and might appreciate the gesture enough to purchase it on their next visit to the grocery store. I think that's brilliant.

What I also thought was interesting was that the gum also promoted the brand's Facebook page in the promotion.

Happened to be in the same restaurant again (surprised?) and when we received our salad order, the fork package included a sample of soft, dental-friendly toothpicks which "remove food easily and discreetly" along with a discount coupon. Another great product sample tie-in!

How could you place your next promotional product in a location that is a natural tie-in? How could you reach out to complementary businesses to explore similar cooperative advertising efforts?

Auto services or insurance. Travel coffee tumblers with your logo could be given to drive-thru customers of a local coffeehouse.

Colleges. Promotional music download cards promoting classes to purchasers of MP3 players at an electronics retailer

And here's a not-so-perfect marriage of promotion and placement.

I arrived at Chicago's Midway airport to head to Minneapolis. It had been a while since I had to travel by air. Most trips were driving distance.

So I arrived at the TSA security check and was surprised to see, in the bottom of the bin that held your belongings, advertising for a major online shoe retailer. Noticed this advertising again on another trip to Philadelphia.

Hmmm...

Okay, I understand the connection with shoes. You're putting your shoes in the bin and you see advertising for shoes. But why are you putting your shoes in there? You're putting them in there because you're going through an airport security check, truly an annoying experience that is now our post-9/11 reality. So even though it's relevant, it also has negative connotations.

So a couple of tips for partner promotions...

Keep It Relevant and Positive. Make sure the promotion is not only relevant, but that the connection between partners, products, and placement is positive. Could be brand and image damaging for both parties.

Establish Procedures and Expectations Upfront. Dates, times and methods of distribution, who will receive the items, and reporting and tracking procedures must be spelled out in advance to prevent misunderstanding and wasted marketing dollars.

Make It Win-Win-Win. Any promotion of this type must be a win for all three parties involved. It must be an item that customers would actually use or want. Your partner now can offer a little something extra that other competitors may not, giving them an advantage. And you get in front of an audience you want.

EVENTS

CHAPTER 18:
5 Ways to Ditch Dreaded Trade Show Promotional Product Thieves

She's hovering around your booth. Big bags. Zero eye contact. In fact, eyes are focused about three feet off the floor, scanning your tables and displays. Eureka! Found your stash of promotional products. Then the dreaded question, *"Is this free?"* You've just been approached by a trade show promotional product thief, a show attendee who is there only to collect your promotional products and not your business card.

Every trade show has them, but some more than others. These thieves are more prevalent in consumer shows, but have been spotted at business-to-business events as well. They are there to swipe as much "free stuff" as they can for their personal use and usually have no intention, authority, ability, or need to buy what you sell. Plus, it's likely they wouldn't refer business to you either. Some of these petty thieves are courteous enough to ask for the items, as in the scenario above. Others grab bunches of giveaways, stash them in a bag, and dash to the next booth.

Trade show promotional product thieves waste your money! They are also a distraction that can keep you from identifying and spending time with valuable trade show visitors. But how can you ditch them? Try these strategies:

1. Make 'Em Earn It. Post a sign that show visitors will receive a free item if they fill out a survey, participate in a game, listen to a presentation, etc. Make them do something that helps you, such as collecting survey data. Chances are they are not going to want to waste time doing what you ask and move on.

2. Make 'Em Wait. Think about offering a freebie that you send after the show. Like with making them earn your giveaway, this delays the instant gratification of grabbing the goods. As well, it gives you a great follow-up opportunity for those show visitors that are truly qualified.

3. Prep Booth Personnel to Weed Out, Not Give Out. Booth personnel, especially if sales is not their main job or they haven't been trained properly, fall into the habit of giving a freebie to everyone that wanders in the booth. They feel that giving out all the giveaways that were shipped to the booth is doing the right thing and getting the word out. Train your booth personnel to qualify, qualify, qualify! Preparing a script or list of questions to quickly qualify booth visitors will help. If the visitor qualifies and provides complete follow-up information, he's eligible to receive a giveaway. If not, train booth personnel to politely send the thieves on their way.

4. Don't Put a Table in Front of the Booth. Not only does a table in the front of a booth discourage interaction with valuable show visitors, it makes promotional product theft a crime of opportunity. If you have a stash of giveaways just sitting on the edge of your table, what's to stop a trade show thief from grabbing a bunch and stuffing them in a bag? If you use a table, place it at the back of the booth with your booth personnel stationed in front of it. Similarly, don't place giveaways in a bin at the front of your display. Too easy for a thief to grab and go.

5. Only Exhibit at Shows that Reach Your Target Audience. When considering exhibiting at a particular event, take time to carefully evaluate the target audience and how show visitors will be invited to the event. Highly qualified attendees are there to do business; the freebies are just a bonus, making thieves less prevalent. If it is a free event open to the public without qualification, you can expect more trade show promotional product thieves in attendance. If the type of business you are in requires attendance at public events such as home shows, utilize the above strategies to reduce loss.

CHAPTER 19:
3 Ways to Avoid the
"Can I Have One For My Kid?"
Problem

A trade show visitor walks up to you, points to one of your promotional products, and asks *"Can I have one of these for my kid?"* Or maybe you're meeting with a client and upon handing him your cool new promotion, he exclaims, *"My kid will love this!"* Your heart sinks as you realize that this promotion will not be used for its intended purpose which is to sell your product, service or cause. Worse yet is that those marketing dollars are being wasted to provide a child with a plaything.

There are also some additional issues that come into play (pun intended!) with these scenarios. Though these items are not intended for children, they are now going to be given to children, opening up an additional layer of consumer product safety concerns.

Can you avoid this problem? Even though whether someone gives an item to a child or not is out of your control, there are some things you can do to make it less of an issue.

1. Select Age and Purpose Appropriate Promotional Products. Select items that adults use. Chances are children are not going to be too interested in items such as auto travel mugs, writing portfolios, and adult-size clothing. Look for items that relate to your marketing purpose or event to help guide you.

2. Avoid "Cute" if Giving to Adults. This is where the trouble really starts. In particular, stress balls available in a myriad of cute characters and shapes are problematic. These are not toys and should not be given to young children! They are not required to be made or imprinted with kid-friendly materials. Bits of them can also be worked off, presenting a swallowing or choking hazard. Same principle for stuffed toys, model cars, novelty pens, and the like.

3. Select Safer Products. Unsure of in what hands your item will end up? Are you actually giving to children as a way to endear yourself to the parents? Select an item that complies with safety standards for non-toxic materials or would not present other hazards by nature. For example, coloring books can be a safer choice, especially looking for those which are identified as using non-toxic inks. Ask your promotional product distributor for details on particular products.

Don't let your promotional product end up in the hands of little ones who have no ability to buy from you! This will save you marketing dollars and will help make your promotions more effective.

CHAPTER 20:
The Promo Is Right: Attract Trade Show Attendees by Making Your Booth a Game Show

You've seen it at every trade show or expo. The 10' x 10' booth with a table of brochures and business cards and a fishbowl to collect business cards for a drawing. Oh yeah, that's special.

Now imagine this. You're walking down a trade show aisle and you hear a clicking sound along with laughs and cheers. And everyone seems to be heading to or hovering around the booth where these sounds are coming from. What is going on? A game...a real, live game activity that can help exhibitors engage with their audiences and encourage them to spend more time and, we hope, more money as a result.

Today, a lot of electronic, location-based games are making their mark as booth traffic generators. This is a great development, especially since these games can begin prior to the show visitors ever entering the door.

But on site, there is something special about a real live game that gets people involved. Why? Simply, the more senses you can engage—sight, sound, touch, taste— the more you can engage your audience.

Plus, by only handing out your promotional products to those who participate in your booth game, you can gain some control over your giveaway budget, too. Make 'em earn it!

So let's look at some choices you can use to make your exhibit say *"Come on down!"*

Prize/Roulette Wheels. Clicking sound helps attract visitors. Plus, many of them have customizable inserts for segments on the wheel.

Bean Bag Toss. Gets people moving and engages touch as they throw the bean bags toward the target.

Plinko. Yes, just like you've seen on the game shows. Visitors drop the pucks to see if they win a prize.

All of these can be used for trade shows, fundraisers, parties, grand openings, open houses, or any event where you want to create a fun and engaging atmosphere.

CHAPTER 21:
3 Exit Strategies to Green
Your Trade Show

Ah, the irony! While a presentation drones on about the evils of plastic water bottles and what should be done about it, attendees at a green new product showcase search for a place to pitch their now empty plastic water bottles. A showcase host replies, *"You know, we hadn't thought about that. Just throw them in the regular trash."*

In case you're wondering, yes, this really happened.

Making your trade show or event greener is a start-to-finish affair. What we'll be looking at here are "exit strategies" you can use to make sure your green efforts don't go walking out the door when your event ends.

1. Bins for Used Lanyards and Name Badges at Exit. Unless the lanyard is super-cool or your event is attended by those who need them for their security badges, it is unlikely that event attendees will ever use them again in the future. Same goes for the plastic badge holders. Why not collect them at the event exit and reuse them for next time? This will not only help the earth, but will save you money since you can buy less for the next event. (See additional lanyard tips later in this book.)

2. Bins for Plastic, Paper, and Aluminum Waste at Exit. The amount of these waste materials generated at events can be huge. With still low recycling rates at the individual level, chances are the pile of paper, plastic containers, and cans will promptly be pitched into the straight-to-landfill waste stream in a hurry once it leaves the building. Tap in to people's desire to unload unnecessary weight at the end of an event and provide separated recycling bins at the exit. Unless you plan to haul it away yourself, this effort will have to be coordinated with the event facility for pick-up.

3. Recycle or Ship Back Show Materials. It's the last few hours of an event and what do you see? Booth personnel scrambling to get rid of show materials so they don't have to pack, ship or drag them back home. What a waste on multiple levels! If you are stuffing brochures or promotional products into the hands of unwilling show visitors, where do you think those items will end up? Of course, in the trash, likely as soon as they leave the show. These materials will also likely end up in the landfill-bound trash, not recycling bin. If you unnecessarily hand out show materials, you will probably have to reorder or reprint them for another event. So you have increased costs for the earth and your marketing budget. Plan in advance how you will handle the return or recycling of unused show materials and advise your booth personnel of procedures.

CHAPTER 22:
Why You Need TSA Friendly
Promotional Products for Trade Shows

Just one more monkey wrench in the tradeshow life! With increased security at airports, there are certainly some items that you won't want to distribute at shows where you know a majority of people will be using air transportation. Why? If they get confiscated as contraband, there go your marketing dollars into the hands of the TSA (Transportation Security Administration). Yes, I'm sure the TSA is quite anxious to get your branded promo and buy from you. Not!

What might some of those prohibited items be (as of the initial writing of this book)?

- *Pocket knives or box cutters, although they can go on as checked baggage.*
- *Scissors with tips or blades over 4 inches. Smaller than that can go on in checked baggage.*
- *Tools such as screwdrivers or wrenches greater than 7 inches in length. Smaller than that can go on in checked baggage.*

- *Any liquids or gels over 3.4 ounces (100ml). I'm still wondering how they came up with the 3.4 ounce limit, aren't you?*
- *Sports equipment such as bats, hockey sticks, and golf clubs (although they can be checked).*
- *Lighters that are not in a DOT (Department of Transportation)-approved container. Filled lighters CANNOT go in checked baggage.*

Visit the TSA website for more information on prohibited items for air travel.

I always get a chuckle when I look through the list of TSA-prohibited items, many of which you can bring on a plane as checked baggage. Glad to know I can bring my brass knuckles, sword, cattle prod, spear gun, and throwing stars in my checked baggage. Whew! I thought my vacation was going to be a bummer. (Insert canned laughter here.)

So what might you consider as promotional products for shows or events where many will be using air transport?

If you have an event that attracts a ton of people who are on the go constantly, sometimes providing them with items to make the journey easier are appreciated...***but only if it fits within your marketing objectives.*** For example, if you have an event that attracts a lot of travelers and you are in the travel arena yourself, TSA-friendly reusable bags with refillable containers (green idea, too!) would be a good choice. Hand sanitizers in small bottles or sprays are also an option. Or maybe something that helps speed up the process upon landing such as luggage wraps that help identify baggage.

I would say the majority of promotional products are TSA-compliant or can be air transported if checked. But to help your promo avoid being an addition to the TSA confiscated bin, definitely steer clear of pocket knives, sharp tools or objects, lighters, and beverages (such as bottled water).

The whole TSA screening experience is annoying enough for most travelers. Don't add to it by providing promo that will delay the process or have to be surrendered.

GREEN

CHAPTER 23:
Eco Friendly Definitions

Before we get too far discussing green promotional product issues, let's review the key terms you'll need to know to make educated buying decisions.

All definitions are arranged in alphabetical order and do not suggest ranking or priority.

Biodegradable. Product containing material that will naturally dissolve or disintegrate when exposed to weather elements or when placed in landfill/composting conditions. Usually this term refers to materials that either do this naturally or are enhanced to degrade within a short period of time (could be less than 5 or 10 years in some cases). Biodegradable products are typically made from plant or animal matter (see also degradable). Helps eliminate buildup of waste material in landfills.

Carbon Footprint. Measurement of the level of carbon produced by the manufacture, distribution, use, and disposal of a product. Carbon levels can also be measured for events and personal lifestyle. See also *offsets.*

Degradable. Product that will disintegrate when exposed to elements (rain, sunlight, etc.) or when deposited into landfills. While all materials are degradable given time (hundreds or thousands or years for some plastics), usually this term refers to materials that either do this naturally or are enhanced to degrade within a short period of time (could be less than 5 or 10 years in some cases). Degradable plastics may be made of petroleum products enhanced with additives to shorten degradation time or to degrade into more earth-friendly substances (see also *biodegradable*). Helps eliminate buildup of waste material in landfills.

Eco-friendly. Term loosely used to describe any product, process, or person that helps save energy, eliminate waste, or prevent harm to people or the planet.

Fair Trade. A method of doing business that seeks to: pay fair prices/wages and benefits for products and services; provide safe and healthy working and living conditions; insists on accountability; and, promotes environmental responsibility. This is of particular concern in developing nations which have suffered exploitation. Fair trade policies prohibit the use of child, forced, or prison labor in the manufacture of goods.

Natural. Material or product derived from a plant or animal source. May or may not be organic. See *organic* definition below.

Offsets. A donation made by a company to balance any environmentally damaging effects of their manufacturing, business activities, or event, particularly carbon emissions. For example, a manufacturer may purchase credits for their excessive carbon footprint which would go towards environmentally supportive efforts such as wind or solar energy projects.

Organic. Material or product derived from a plant or animal source using organic methods. Organic methods do not use chemical herbicides, pesticides, or genetically modified organisms (GMO). They may use energy and water saving equipment and processes. Organic materials cannot be processed using the same facilities and equipment used for non-organic methods. To be labeled as organic, material or product must be verified by a third party such as the USDA (U.S. Dept. of Agriculture). Organic materials cannot be processed using the same facilities and equipment used for non-organic methods.

Pre-Consumer. Waste material resulting from manufacturing processes that has not yet been used or consumed by an end user.

Post-Consumer. Waste material that has been used at least once by an end user.

Recyclable. Product or material that can be melted, shredded, disassembled, or otherwise broken down and remanufactured for use in another product. These can include glass, plastic, fabric, wood, metals, and paper. Plastics are usually rated with a recycling symbol to indicate chemical composition and/or recyclability. Helps divert volume of waste going into landfills.

Recycled. Product or material made from a waste product. Content can include pre-consumer or post-consumer content or both.

Renewable. Can describe a product, material, or energy source that can be easily replenished, with low or no environmental damage or cost, when depleted.

Reusable. Any product that can be used more than once. The more times it can be used, the longer it takes to make its way to a landfill. May also be made of recyclable material which can further divert materials from landfills.

Socially Responsible. A broad term to describe the labor policies used in the manufacture of a product or material. Can also refer to a manufacturer's commitment to community development or charitable efforts.

Sustainable. Synonymous with renewable. Usually refers to products, materials, or energy sources that are easily replenished, with low or no environmental damage or cost, when depleted.

Third Party Verification. Government and non-government organizations can provide certification that a specific methodology or policy was adhered to during the manufacture of a specific product. Labor policies and organic farming methods are two areas that can be verified. One such certifying organization is the U.S. Department of Agriculture (USDA).

CHAPTER 24:
Eco Friendly Promotional Product Shopping Guidelines (or Buy This, Not That)

Is there some sort of ranking of eco friendliness? Yes. When shopping for promotional products that are better for our planet, here are, in order, the factors to consider:

Recycled (with Post-Consumer Content). These products truly help close the green loop by keeping waste products out of landfills and reducing the amount of virgin material being created from resources that are not easily renewable such as petroleum.

Recycled (with Pre-Consumer Content). Well, at least these products keep the waste from manufacturing out of landfills. Has been going on for a long time as a standard manufacturing process to reduce waste and costs. So the product you're buying may already have been a "recycled" product. Now manufacturers are just telling you about it.

Biodegradable. In theory, everything is biodegradable; it just depends on how many years it takes and what it biodegrades into. If a product is labeled as "biodegradable," it typically is made from a substance that will break down, dissolve or disintegrate within a short period of time when compared to standard plastics which could survive for millennia. Some will degrade if exposed to elements or landfill conditions in as less than a decade. Also, biodegradable products are usually formulated to degrade into either non-harming or even beneficial residues. See specific product info for details since not all biodegradable products are made from the same material or biodegrade in the same way. Only issue with biodegradable is that it does require the continuous manufacture of new material, even if it is eco friendly or sustainable.

Recyclable. These products may or may not include recycled content, but can be thrown into the recycling stream (where facilities exist) and be resurrected into other products, again, closing the green loop.

Reusable. One of the weakest of the eco-friendly claims, but does carry some weight if the product typically is a throwaway that now can be used again. If purchasing a reusable promotional product, one that is also recyclable when its reusing days are over is the most earth-friendly choice.

Buying Local. With less fuel needed to transport your purchase to you, you help conserve oil resources. However, in the promotional products arena, your distributor may live next door to you, but the product you purchase from them may be coming from across the country. Plus, inputs to the manufacture of the product can be from anywhere in the world. A difficult to qualify eco friendly claim.

Socially Responsible. Uses unionized, local/home country, or fair trade labor. Also may tout charitable donations made with each purchase. Not so much an eco friendly choice (except if a donation is made to an environmental cause) as a feel good or community driven choice.

CHAPTER 25:
4 Greener Promotional Product Decorating Options

You've selected an eco-friendly promotional product that's recycled, biodegradable, recyclable, or at least reusable. But doesn't the imprinting process use petroleum-based inks which are bad for the environment? Yes, that may be true. So to make your choice greener all the way around, inquire whether any of these greener decorating options might be available:

1. Laser Etching. This inkless laser process etches your logo into the surface of a product. Basically the top layer of the surface is etched away, leaving the base surface to show through in the shape of your logo. Depending of the top and base surface colors, this may leave a very visible or a very subtle imprint. For example, if the top surface is a blue painted coating and the base surface is a silvery metallic, it will leave a silvery and very visible logo. However, if the surface is an unpainted metal, it may leave a logo that is substantially the same color as the product, but with a slightly different texture. Laser etching is generally done on metals and glass.

Produces a sophisticated look with high imprint durability.

2. Debossing. Another inkless option, debossing uses heat to impress your logo into the surface of an item. Like laser etching, this will leave a subtle and sophisticated tone-on-tone look. Generally debossing is available on thicker surfaces that would respond to heat. Padded writing portfolios would be a prime example. It is also being used on recycled cardboard and leather surfaces. Offers high imprint durability.

3. Embroidery. While some of the dyes used in embroidery threads may or may not be totally green or organic, it is another option that does not employ application of petroleum-based inks.

4. Water-Based Inks. Mainly for promotional T-shirts and fabric items, water-based inks are now available.

CHAPTER 26:
Do Fair Trade Promotional Products Exist?

Where was it made? Who made it? How was it made? What's in it? These are going to become very important questions as the concern over fair trade issues continues to grow, especially as the more socially conscious Generation Y demographic begins to have greater influence in the marketplace. To clarify, fair trade policies prohibit the use of child, forced or prison labor in the manufacture of goods, seek to pay fair wages, and emphasize accountability and environmental sustainability. This is a critical issue in much of the developing world.

In the area of promotional products (imprinted pens, mugs, T-shirts, etc.), fair trade choices are limited and often not clearly identified. This is not to say that those products that do not come with fair trade in their description don't qualify. In fact, many of them do. However, at present, it needs to be confirmed on a case by case basis and cannot be assumed. Fair trade certifications are available, but promotional products do not clearly fall under one specific program, making it confusing for both distributors and their customers.

One way for marketers to ensure they are buying fair trade promotional products is to limit choices to those made in countries with established fair labor standards such as the United States. That opens up some more options, but still quite limited. In a review of the Advertising Specialty Institute ESP Online database (as of the initial edition of this book), around 10% or less of products in major promotional product categories such as pens, mugs, and T-shirts are USA made. There is also the chance that some of the materials or components used in manufacture were sourced from outside the United States; however, to be classified as "made in the USA," the imported materials or parts cannot be a significant portion of the whole.

What should a marketer do to make more socially conscious choices?

Ask! Discuss your fair trade purchasing objectives with your promotional product distributor or marketing consultant. Ask for verification and/or certification that can confirm the origin or compliance of the product.

Specify Made in the USA or Fair Trade Nation. If unsure that your product choice or its country of origin qualifies, select an option that is made in the United States. The United States has well-established fair labor laws and enforcement in place. Again, if in doubt, ask!

CHAPTER 27:
How to Green Up Promotional T-Shirt Buying with Life Cycle Assessment

Have you ever thought about what happens to your imprinted T-shirt after your event? It's a good question and one that you really need to think about BEFORE buying.

Ideally, of course, you'd like to think that your T-shirt will be worn by recipients as they work out, shop at the store, or go to other events. Unfortunately, that's not the case.

Here are some of the more popular post-event lives for imprinted T-shirts:

Pajamas. Yes, they will have lots of market exposure while people sleep. Not!

Car Wash Rags. Especially if they're white and don't have a lot of printing on them.

Gardening/Housework Attire. It's not appropriate enough to wear out on the street. So it's okay to mess it up while doing dirty work.

Charity/Resale Donation. Your T-shirt could be going straight to the donation bin after your event.

Let's take a moment to talk about charity donations. It surprises many people to learn that charities don't always sell these castoffs in their resale stores. Items that are not considered suitable for sale on a resale level are often sold by weight to jobbers who sell them to a variety of markets both here and abroad.

Don't be disheartened by the fate of your event T-shirt being shredded for other use or going somewhere other than to a needy person here or in another country. In the promotional arena, there is a new market for recycled fiber fabrics. Both cottons and synthetic fibers are being repurposed into new T-shirts and fleece items.

Knowing the life cycle (and afterlife) of that promotional T-shirt project you're planning is key to making a greener purchase. Specifically, you need to assess:

Potential Lifetime. How long, in terms of months or years, would you expect recipients to wear it? Will they wear it at the event and send it directly to the charity bin? Some of this can be determined by the quality of the shirt you choose. Higher quality or very comfortable ones, regardless of imprint, can become favorites. I've received some at athletic events that I immediately sent to the donation pile. The fabrics were cheap, itchy, wrinkly, had an imprint that used so much ink I thought I was wearing a plastic bag, or, in the case of a "tech" fabric, so hot I sweat in them instantly. Goodbye! Also, to help extend the shirt's life post-donation, opt for limiting imprint areas to expand the useful fabric area. Imprinted areas are often unusable except for scrap fiber.

Your Recipients. Are your recipients T-shirt wearers? I've done a lot of running events and I've observed that a lot of the runners are very unlikely to wear the event shirt at the race. Very competitive runners or athletes do NOT typically wear them on race day. They wear their training gear or, what I call, "good luck wear." They may wear the event shirt after the event, but typically not for training. Really the only ones they want are those for high profile competitive running events such as marathons. It becomes a badge of honor they'll be proud to display! But for fun runs and community type events, maybe not so much (a box of free energy bars might be more appreciated). By contrast, at a fun run/walk, you may have a lot of families where a wearable freebie might help stretch the clothing budget for kids. Plus, kids might want to show off that they were cool enough to participate. So, yes, they want them.

Collectible Potential. How much do you think you could get on eBay for a vintage 1970s rock concert T-shirt? Probably a good buck! Is the promotional shirt you're buying going to promote a once-in-a-lifetime experience? Does it commemorate an up-and-coming artist that could make it valuable in the future? This may be difficult to assess. Generally, though, the higher profile the event, performer, or place visited, the more collectible market value the shirt may have down the road.

Extended Promotional Value. Shirts which promote a continuing effort, such as awareness campaigns, may have an extended life after an initial event. In this case you would be well advised to select a wear-worthy choice that is comfortable and better quality to foster continued post-event wear.

Supply Chain. Sometimes this is tricky. Most promotional online vendors rarely, if ever, identify the country of origin for T-shirts. It can vary widely from product to product. As well, in the case of overseas production, source country could change rapidly should the manufacturer move operations to circumvent quota issues. I have seen T-shirt samples of the exact same shirt style that have different countries of origin on each. If fair trade issues are a concern, stick with USA-made T-shirts. Should you be more concerned about a greener fabric content—for example, you don't want cotton made with pesticides or herbicides—then stick with organics. To be labeled organic, it must be processed separately.

Whew! That was quite a journey. Bottom line? You need to think outside the event when purchasing.

CHAPTER 28:
When Eco Friendly Promotional Products Don't Work

With our society's emphasis on green issues, it might seem unthinkable that there would be occasions not to use eco-friendly promotional products. But there are.

Let's look at one in particular. An office equipment dealer received most of his promotional products from a manufacturer he represented. One of the products was reusable grocery totes. Nice gesture. But did it support his efforts of selling office equipment? No. Hope these bags aren't residing in a landfill somewhere.

What are the occasions when an eco friendly choice is not appropriate?

When It Doesn't Align With Your Product or Service. It seems that everyone is giving our reusable tote and grocery bags these days. Let's say you develop software for manufacturing, Does it make sense to have your customers flaunting your name and website in the local grocery store? Probably not. You've just wasted an important "green" resource: your money. That being said, when you do find a product that is appropriate for your business, seeking a greener version of it is the right thing to do.

When Your Company Has Not Made a Commitment to Green Initiatives. Integrity alert! Using eco friendly promotional products when your company has not yet made a commitment to going greener sends mixed signals to your customers and prospects, decreasing your trust factor.

When You Don't Really Need to Buy Anything. A key earth-friendly principle is to reduce your consumption. If you do have less environmentally friendly promotional products in your supply room, don't run out to buy a greener product just to feel good. Use up what you have and then restock with a greener alternative when you run out.

CHAPTER 29:
Yuck! A Dark Side of
Going Green at Events

I had quite a revelation about tradeshow and event lanyards at a conference. What I learned is that many people often enjoy getting them as souvenirs. So let's call them badges (pun intended) of honor. But for event veterans (like me), I don't need another lanyard for sure!

And for those in the events world who want to go greener for both the environment and their budgets, recycling lightly used lanyards at future events seems like a great idea.

But while at an Event Camp conference, I was chatting some of my pals about greener meetings. Mentioned the idea of collecting and recycling lanyards at future events. There was an "eeewww" response, although, in theory, this sounded like a logical solution. Makeup, oils, personal products and more can accumulate on them making some give pause to using a recycled lanyard. Also, washing them is either not possible or practical. Truly a dark side to going green for this particular item at meetings.

Guess that scenario really never crossed my mind, probably because I'm not too much of a germaphobe (I have two big always-a-mess dogs). But I have to realize that there are others not so inclined.

So now what? Are we going to have to continue to buy new lanyards for every event, only to have them pitched into the garbage after maybe 10-20 hours of wear? Hmm...what to do?

Here are some thoughts...

Still Collect and Recycle, But Offer New. I'm going to guess that some people are like me and using a recycled lanyard doesn't faze them. What event and tradeshow planners can do is still collect the lanyards and offer a recycled one to attendees, but also have a stash of brand new ones for those who are more sensitive on this issue or those who collect them as souvenirs.

B.Y.O.B.L. No, not Bring Your Own Booze & Liquor (although some might). How about Bring Your Own Badge/Lanyard? No doubt, if you have a gathering of regular conference goers, they have quite a stockpile of these little-used gizmos. Many may also use them every day on the job. Give them a bit of a reward if they agree to bring and use their own badge and lanyard. Less cost for you and the planet. Key to making this work is communicating this to attendees in advance.

CHAPTER 30:
How Green Are Promotional Products Now?

Hard to believe that it's been decades since the very first Earth Day in 1970. So where do I see the green movement, especially as it relates to promotional products and marketing?

Green Dollar Values Still Trump Green Values. I still see lots of people choosing green dollar values over green values. What's interesting is that even when times are economically better, people weren't hopping onto the green bandwagon in droves. Unless it's a huge deal for the company, such as if they are working on achieving a certain environmental standard, it's a nice to do, not a have to do, effort for promotional products. As well, prices are still higher for many more eco friendly products, although some are getting closer to their standard product cousins.

Small Efforts Are Gaining Some Ground. Maybe it's just choosing a reusable product over a disposable one. These small, easy to do efforts do seem to be gaining a foothold.

The Green Excuse for Not Marketing. This is hilarious. Sometimes when I'm soliciting promo business, I get the *"we're going green so we're not buying anything"* excuse. Yes, excuse. Please, people, don't paint your non-activity as going green if you're reason for not buying is the other green (cash). Be authentic!

Digital Marketing is Seen as a Panacea, But There's a Catch. Event and tradeshow people are flocking to digital marketing strategies such as those that use QR codes or mobile apps. But there's a big catch: You've got to get people to buy in. At a number of events, I've included a big QR code in my booth. I can probably count on one hand the people who understood what it was or how to use it. Many times, I'd have to show them how to download a scanning app. And I really, really hate wasting my selling time showing someone how to use their own mobile device. Often what I hear is *"I just bought this phone and I have no idea how to use it."* So I use these tools carefully, tailoring it to the anticipated audience.

Promotional USB Drives Will Continue to Lose Favor. On a related digital marketing note, promotional USB drives will continue to lose favor as mobile apps and more powerful smartphones saturate the market.

Green & Gross. While many people are willing to reuse containers, clothing, and more at home, they are not so willing to share or reuse personal items at events. This necessitates offering both recycled and new, as well as having to deal with cleaning and/or storing recycled items.

SWAG ORDERING HOW-TO ADVICE

CHAPTER 31:
Understanding the Buying Process

"We'd like you to order up some new company T-shirts for us." You need to get up to speed on buying this type of thing...fast!

Here is some important real world knowledge about the promotional product buying process...

Prices and Products are Not the Same as at Target. Newer and less experienced buyers are usually sticker-shocked at how much an item will cost when purchased for promotional purposes. *"But I can get a Hanes T-shirt at Target for $3"* they muse when their distributor quotes a price of $6 for what they feel is the same shirt with just some printing on it. In some cases it might be the same shirt or something very similar.

Here's the situation. Large retailers are buying product by the truckloads. Notice that it is truckloads with a "s." They have huge centralized buying forces that negotiate based on volume and many other factors such as shipping. Your 144 piece order is a short, special order run even for the distributor and his suppliers. Plus, you are buying occasionally and they usually don't know when your next order might come in. Thus the higher pricing to cover their costs to hand hold you through your order without guarantees for future business. Additionally, your distributor or decorator incurs costs to set up presses and process your order. These are also built into your price.

You Need "Good" Art. If you email a JPEG file of your logo to your promotional product distributor, first he'll just shake his head and say, *"Not another one."* In this situation, your distributor may ask you to provide electronic artwork in a "vector" format such as Encapsulated Postscript (.eps) or Adobe Illustrator (.ai). These formats provide clean-edged art that is required for imprinting and can usually be provided by your company's graphic designer. Alternatively, they may charge you an art clean-up fee to make it print-ready.

Your Distributor is Not Printing Your Product in His Office or Basement. Promotional products are typically imprinted at large facilities that can handle orders of hundreds or thousands pieces each. Your distributor is often not printing them for you at his or her company. So suggesting that you can pick up your order at your distributor's office to save some time or shipping costs will not be met with a positive response.

Shipping and Handling Costs and Issues Can be Huge. After the product price sticker shock, shipping and handling fees are often the aftershock. There are multiple issues.

First, a single tote bag, T-shirt, or mug may seem like a small item. Now multiply that by 1,000 or more. The sheer physical volume of a large quantity of promotional products can overwhelm your office or dock. Also, thousands of boxed up pieces could be of significant weight, maybe even into the hundreds or thousands of pounds. Ask your distributor for information on the shipment size and weight and how it will be delivered to you so you can plan accordingly. While you're at it, ask them for an estimated shipping cost, too.

Second, expedited shipping is very, very, very expensive! In many cases, your product will not be shipping from the person or company from which are buying. It may be shipping across the country to your door. Many distributors do their best to look for the closest suppliers to shorten shipping time and cost. So allow for sufficient time to get the product produced plus the time to ship to you.

Now that you know more about the promotional products industry and the buying process, you won't be sending out a newbie alert when you contact your distributor.

CHAPTER 32:
To Logo or Not to Logo?

"I'm one of the sponsors at a community event next week. The event organizers want me to send them a logo for the signage. But I don't have one. What should I do? Should I go out and get one? Or should I just find some clip art to send them?" Got that phone call from an accounting friend of mine. Her situation is not unique. If you're a small business, you might be able to sympathize with that.

Investing in an official logo for your company is a big step in your business' development. You'll be using it for years and it is an investment that may cost you several hundred to maybe a couple thousand dollars. But when it is right to take that big step?

Some image development professionals will tell you that you should invest in a logo as soon as you start your business. For a very small business, I think that might be an expense that can be delayed. As you develop as a business owner, your needs will develop and change. Continually changing your logo to fit your growing business is a huge cash outlay which will affect your early profitability. Better to select a common basic font (such as Arial/Helvetica or Times Roman) for your company name that can be used for early advertising or websites. Use your company name and tagline (placing the tagline in italics helps set it off from the company name) the same way every time, everywhere. On the other hand, if your company, right out of the gate, is a large one that will have a major public presence, it is worth the extra expense and effort.

The Clip Art Logo Problem. While you're waiting to grow to the point where you can afford a logo identity package, do not use clip art images as your logo. One, it is usually illegal. Many clip art providers expressly prohibit the use of their images for this purpose. Why? Logo and brand identity development is a unique skill and commands higher fees from clients. Say you downloaded some clip art image for one dollar and you use it in your logo. That is a missed opportunity cost for the designer. Hey, graphic designers who sell on stock artwork sites are often small businesses too. Would you be willing to offer what you do for only a buck or two?

Two, even if the use of the clip art in a logo is legal, someone else has certainly used it for their logo too. So much for creating a unique identity!

The Ink Jet Printer/Online Business Card Problem. I don't know about you, but I can always tell when someone has printed her business cards at home on her ink jet printer. Welcome to Amateur Hour! If you are not willing to invest even $50 or $100 to get some "real" business cards, chances are you're not really ready to be in business either.

Then there are those that use an online site that offers free or really cheap business cards. These are usually co-branded cards on which the provider's name and yours appears. *"What a deal,"* you think. I do not recommend this ever. Why? First, you are giving the provider a ton of free advertising for their website or other services. They should be providing them to you for free! Second, go to any networking event. Chances are you will run into someone who is using the same design that you are. In the inevitable quick run through of business cards that happens after a networking event, yours might get pitched because it looks like another from a person that didn't impress them.

When you first start your business, a great logo alternative is a picture of YOU! Use it on your business cards and website. In fact, don't be afraid to use it in your marketing materials whether you're just starting out or are brilliantly successful after several years. People buy from people, not text or logos.

CHAPTER 33:
Tips for Hiring a Graphic Designer for Your Logo

Once you've decided to make the leap to invest in a logo or brand identity package, here are tips to save you money and get a logo that will serve you well into the future:

Do Not Have a Family Member or Friend Create the Logo. Of all the logo disasters I've encountered in my networking, this is the most prevalent. Unless your family member or close friend is a true professional graphic and identity designer—and even then, I would not only recommend it with caution—hire someone that is a "stranger" of sorts. They will be looking at your image from that all-important outsider viewpoint.

Do Not Barter for Logo Design. A networking contact is a "graphic designer" (or thinks he is). He needs the service or products you provide and offers to create your logo for either free or for a dramatically discounted rate. Here's what happens. You provide your products or services. He creates a logo (or several) that just don't work for you. Now you're stuck. Should you use the miserable mess he's created? Or should you use another designer? If you use the mess, you mess up your brand. If you don't use it, you will essentially be paying double for it since you've already given away your time, talent, products, and maybe even income.

If You Don't Like What They've Created, Say So. Anything that involves creativity involves judgment. And everyone has different tastes. While you don't want to become a prima donna client, if you don't like what's been created, tell your designer. Be specific about why you don't like it and make constructive comments as to how your designer can change it to meet your needs.

Insist on Receiving a Complete Set of Electronic Logo Files. Your designer must provide you with a complete set of electronic logo files that you can provide to printers, web designers, and places where you advertise. The main file that you will need is a vector format (non-pixel) rendering of your logo; this is typically an Adobe Illustrator (.ai) or Encapsulated Postscript (.eps) file with clean, smooth edges on all elements. If you do not have a program that can read these files, ask your designer for an Adobe Reader (.pdf) file to view. This will assure that your logo can be used on items such as promotional products and can be scaled up or down, without distortion, for signage. When viewing the proof the artwork, zoom it up to around 500% to check for the clean edges. If they're ragged, all the designer has done is convert a .jpeg file to .eps and the artwork is not usable in design applications.

In sum, this logo file set will, at minimum, include: 1) Encapsulated Postscript (.eps) file in color; 2)

Encapsulated Postscript (.eps) file in black and white; 3) High-resolution JPEG file; and, 4) Low-resolution JPEG file for use on the web.

Another word of caution: If, in the black and white rendering of your logo, you see any portion that is a shade of gray, reject that logo and tell your designer to render it in solid black. Why? When using this logo for promotional products or signage, gray cannot be imprinted. Imprinting equipment can only see solids and gray is always a "screen," meaning it is a collection of micro dots. The results will either be messy or come out solid anyway. To illustrate, imagine this. Let's say your logo is a black circle on a gray square. When imprinted, all you will see is an almost solid black square which looks nothing like your logo. A good graphic designer will create your logo in solid black and white first, then add color later. Ask for the black and white version before you see it in color so that you can evaluate. Ask for this before the designer begins work. If the designer refuses or tries to tell you that it isn't possible, reject the designer because you will be using the one-color logo more often than you think!

CHAPTER 34:
What is "Good Artwork" for Imprinting?

For it to be "good artwork" for imprinting on promotional products, what's required is "vector" artwork. Vector artwork is created through "mathematically defined" objects, like plotting points and drawing lines between them. The result is clean, crisp graphics that are scalable, meaning that it will look essentially the same whether you use it at 1 inch or 100 inches. The graphic below on the left is a representation of a vector graphic.

On the other hand (and as shown on the right side of the above image), "raster" artwork is a bitmap image. Bitmap images are composed of a checkerboard type grid of squares and are usually used for photographic type images. The resolution is critical to resizing and working with them. Most web type images are 72 pixels per inch (very low resolution) and those used for high resolution printing can be as high as 300 or 600 per inch. If you grab a web image and then zoom in, you can see the squares.

The reason the clean lines are needed is because ink imprinting your logo art is usually done with a silkscreentype process. Think of it as somewhat like a stencil. Now imagine you have to cut the stenciled design using the rough edge graphic shown on the right. Might be less than smooth edges for sure!

Your logo designer should be able to provide you with an Encapsulated Postscript (.eps), Adobe Illustrator (.ai), or a print production quality PDF file that you can pass along to your promotional products distributor. Once you have that, your distributor can easily resize it to whatever imprint size you'll need for your project. Word of caution: Do not try to "convert" a .jpg or .gif file to an .eps or .pdf format, thinking that it will magically turn into production ready artwork. It will not. It just converts the low res file into a file that can be read (not used) as an .eps or print ready .pdf.

If, for some reason, you cannot get a vector art file for your promotional product project, your distributor can usually have it redrawn for you by a graphic artist. This will involve extra expense and time. So investing in hiring a designer to create imprint-ready artwork will save you time and dollars over the years.

CHAPTER 35:
How to Deal With Itsy Bitsy Imprints

You're looking through a promotional product website or catalog and you see a product you're interested in. You imagine your logo emblazoned on it big, bold and beautiful. Then you look at the imprint area which is 3/4" square. What? Yep, that's small, even if it's shown as huge in the extreme close-up photo.

Just to give you a dose of reality, take out a ruler right now and measure off 3/4". Now imagine your logo shrunk down to that size. Is it still legible? In many cases, when logos are shrunk down to less than 1", they become almost unidentifiable except with the use of a magnifying glass.

However, this is the reality you must deal with for many itsy bitsy imprints such as those on golf balls, golf tees and ball markers, pens, keytags, lapel pins, and the like. Sure, today's imprinting technologies, including digital printing, can achieve logo imprints that were next to impossible in years past. But remember that you want your imprint to be identifiable from a normal viewing distance.

So keep these guidelines in mind as you prepare artwork for the itsy bitsy imprint situations:

Ditch Text, Keep Graphic Elements. If you have a logo that includes both graphic elements and text, ditch the text when faced with a small imprint area. I realize that there are logos that are text treatments and do not have any shape elements in them. In that case you might want to just isolate the first letter in your company name or use an acronym. Ask your graphic designer to suggest some alternatives for limited space that maintain your branding.

Only Use Text. This may sound contradictory to the above, but if faced with extreme size limitations, you might opt for just plain text. Your promotional product distributor can provide you with the number of characters that are available for your imprint. For example, one of my regular clients has quite a large logo. When they buy golf tees from me, which have an imprint area of 3/8" x 1-3/8", we opt for the text only option which gives them up to 3 lines of text, 24 characters per line.

Size Matters. While most modern day imprinting processes can produce some amazingly detailed small imprints, there is a limit to how low you can go in terms of text size. Typically, text sizes of 5 to 8 points are about the smallest you can go, but it depends on the imprint area, the surface material it's going on, as well as the ink and equipment being used. Your promotional product distributor can advise you of what's possible.

Choose Product and Imprint Colors to Match Your Branding. So you don't have enough space to use your snazzy full color logo and you have to go with a text-only imprint. Match the product and/or imprint colors you use to blend in with your branding to still get some of the effect.

Contrast Helps. When choosing product and imprint colors, make sure there is sufficient contrast between the two. Helps the readability when the size shrinks.

CHAPTER 36:
How to Imprint QR Codes

QR codes, those checkerboard-like squares also known as 2D codes, are everywhere it seems. On signs, clothing, business cards, heck, even tattoos. The beauty of them is that when scanned by a smartphone, they'll make things happen such as take you to a website, return information, send messages, and more.

But there are some issues with them that you need to be aware of when using them on promotional products...

Size. Though I've tried and used QR codes quite a bit smaller, usually about 1″ square is recommended as a minimum for best scanning ability.

Surface. I've seen some pretty kooky uses of QR codes including knitted and on a waffle (seriously, I just saw that in a presentation). But here's the catch: It must be readable by a smartphone or other reading device. For best scanning, I suggest imprinting on only smooth plastic, paper, painted metal, or flat even surface fabrics.

T-Shirt Issues. Unstretched T-shirt fabric is just fine for imprinting QR codes. But realize that if it is stretched when worn, it may lose scanability. Conversely, if someone tucks the shirt into their jeans, it may scrunch the imprint together and be unreadable. And, please, do not imprint on the front of a shirt. It is especially awkward when women wear them, resulting in a lot of scanning of, well, do I have to explain?

Color and Contrast. You can use colors other than black. But dark colors are suggested. Do not imprint the code in white. It will mess up the reading since what was white is now black and vice versa, a completely different code. I've tried it. On a related issue, make sure there is a definite contrast between the dark and light areas. That's why imprinting on colored surfaces is problematic. There may not be enough contrast between the surface and the code to be readable. So choose white or very light surface colors and dark imprints. On a related note, clear plastic or glass surfaces may also be problematic because of the color and contrast issues; choose white plastic or ceramic instead.

Ink Imprints Recommended. Debossing (impressing your code into a surface) or laser engraving cannot be used successfully for QR codes due to the contrast issue discussed above. And though contrast can be achieved with it, embroidery also has the potential to not be scannable due to uneven surface texture. Ink imprinting on smooth surfaces, please.

Order a Physical Production Sample for Large Orders. Let's call this insurance. When you are investing thousands of dollars in promotional products, it makes sense to do a physical (not virtual!) production sample to see if the artwork will be properly scanable on the surface and in the colors you have chosen. Say it costs you $100-

$200 to do that. Better that than having to pitch at $1,000 to $2,000 order because it doesn't work.

I think people are just enchanted with the technology right now and that the novelty will wear off. Would you want to wear a UPC pricing barcode on your clothing? Probably not. Essentially that's what you're doing when you're sportin' QR codes. Wearing barcodes.

CHAPTER 37:
7 Things You Need to Know When Ordering Imprinted T-Shirts

"Let's get some printed T-shirts for the event." Well, that should be easy, right? Do you want to take a guess at how many choices you have? One of the imprinted apparel industry's leading warehousing suppliers has over 300 different T-shirts in its inventory. 300! Then there are decorating options. Do you want the front or back or both decorated? Maybe the sleeves, too? How many colors should be printed? Overwhelming!

This is where a promotional products marketing consultant can be your best friend. Based on your needs, he or she can help narrow the field and still stay within your budget. Let's dispel one myth right away. There is no such thing as a standard promotional T-shirt. So let's look at what you need to consider when buying.

Fabric Content. 100 percent cotton or a 50/50 blend of cotton and a synthetic fiber are most common. Many people feel that all cotton T-shirts are more comfortable. However, blended fabrics are often less wrinkly and are sometimes softer than all cotton. Time of year and preference of those who will be wearing the shirts will dictate.

Fit. Most men's T-shirts are cut with a boxy shape, making them usable for both sexes. If you do not know how many women and men will be receiving your shirts, opt for the men's cut to cover all bases. Ladies fit shirts vary widely in cut and sizing and are best avoided for new buyers of promotional apparel. Children's sized shirts are also available. But you will have to have a pretty clear idea of the age and sizing you will need when ordering.

Eco Friendly/Fair Trade Options. For markets or groups that are sensitive to eco friendly issues, there are shirts made with organic cotton that does not use pesticides, herbicides, or genetically modified (GMO) seeds. As well, organic farming uses water management as opposed to heavy irrigation. Organic cottons must carry a certification of their organic farming, harvesting, and processing methods. Fair trade selections, some of them also being organic, prohibit the use of child, forced, or prison labor in the manufacture of the materials or the assembly process.

Colors. White is the least expensive choice. Heathers, which are often used in athletic wear, are a middle priced option. Black and colors are most expensive. Your budget will dictate here.

Imprinting. Screen printing is the most common method for decorating promotional T-shirts. One color imprinting is the least expensive since there are additional set-up and running charges for multiple colors. If your logo is multi-colored, have your graphic designer reinterpret the design to black and white art (no gray allowed). Vector art, which is typically an Encapsulated Postscript (.eps) or Adobe Illustrator (.ai) file, is usually required for screen printing. Again, your graphic designer can assist in preparing your artwork.

Imprint Locations. Typically a full front, left chest, or full back imprint are the most commonly used locations. Occasionally, the edges of short sleeves or the full length of a long-sleeve are used. However, be aware that as you add up the locations, your set-up and running charges add up, too. Best to stick with maybe the front and/or back for cost savings. Your promotional products consultant can provide you with artwork sizes to pass along to your graphic designer.

Quantities. While promotional T-shirts can be sold by the single piece or in dozen quantities, they are typically sold by the case size of 72 for best pricing. Some promotional product consultants or decorators will not accept orders less than 72. Quantities less than that may be cost prohibitive for you. Your promotional consultant can help you determine what is possible for you.

CHAPTER 38:
What Does T-Shirt Ounce Weight Mean and Why Is It Important?

If you've ever shopped for promotional imprinted T-shirts, you've likely encountered an ounce weight in a product description such as 5.5 oz., 6.1 oz. or 4.5 oz. Does that mean the shirt weighs that much or what?

Technically, the ounce weight means that a square yard of the T-shirt fabric weighs that many ounces. So for a 6.1 oz. T-shirt, a square yard of the fabric weighs 6.1 oz. As logic would dictate, the heavier the ounce weight, the thicker and heavier the T-shirt.

Ounce weight of a T-shirt is important to know so that you can select a shirt that's appropriate for your marketing purpose. Most standard T-shirts are in the 4.5 oz. to 6 oz. range. Below that, the fabrics are light weight and may not be very durable which might be appropriate for some applications such as one-time event use. Additionally, some lightweight T-shirts are tissue, sheer or fine jersey which are popular for some markets, such as for women's wear. If you're looking for T-shirts that will get heavy wear and tear, such as for uniform or construction use, generally a thicker weight of 6.0 oz. or above would be recommended.

Another reason ounce weight of a T-shirt is important is because it will affect how much it is to ship from your supplier or decorator to you. The heavier the shirts, the heavier the boxes or the more boxes you may have to ship. T-shirts are a heavy promotional item! A regular T-shirt could weigh up to a half pound by itself depending on the fabric and design. Multiply that by hundreds...you get the idea. So unless you're doing a special type of T-shirt, it's generally best to source as close to you as possible to avoid high freight costs which could run into the hundreds of dollars.

CHAPTER 39:
10 Things You Need to Know When Ordering Embroidered Apparel

A polo shirt is a polo shirt. NOT! "Polo shirt" is just a term used to describe a knit shirt that goes over the head and has a collar often used for golf and tennis. So it could be used to describe hundreds and hundreds of different shirts. Then there are both men's and ladies' styles. There are a lot of shirts to choose from!

Adding to the number of styles to choose from, you also need to think about sizes, colors, embroidery, artwork to use...whew, that's a lot of details! So let's break down what information you really need when you are ordering branded apparel for your tradeshow personnel or even for everyday wear.

1. Type of Garment. Do you need polos or woven dress shirts? Either are used for tradeshow and event staff use, although polos tend to be the more comfortable choice.

2. Fabric. How comfortable a shirt or jacket feels is largely determined by the fabric and your group's preferences. "Jersey" has a smooth surface and is used in both polos and T-shirts. "Pique" has a textured surface and is usually a bit heavier than jersey. "Jacquard" has a patterned surface that's knitted in. There are also "performance" fabrics which are designed to release sweat and keep dry—good for golf outings and other warm weather events.

3. Mens, Ladies or Unisex Styles. While many women could wear a mens shirt, a ladies cut shirt has a more flattering fit. If you have a lot of women working at your show or in your office, it is suggested to order styles that have a ladies fit. Looks better for your marketing image, feels better for them.

4. Size. Usually branded wearables are sized in Small, Medium, Large, etc. which are comparable to the same size designations in retail. So do not expect a totally custom fit. If you think sizing may be an issue, order blank samples before ordering your decorated apparel. Even though the samples are non-returnable, if you have a large quantity or dollar value order, it's worth it to be sure.

5. Quantity of Each Size. Get sizes in advance, don't guess! Since I always encourage people to go greener with their promotions, this eliminates the waste of both material and dollars that comes with over-ordering or reordering when you don't know sizes. Plus, by asking your recipients what size they want, it puts the onus on them for selecting a size.

6. Color of Garment. Easy, sort of. Again, if it's critical to match up a shirt color with your logo or theme, might be wise to get a sample in advance to check.

7. Location of Embroidery. For polos, woven shirts and jackets, embroidering the logo on the left chest is typical. Why? Because you usually put your name or name tag on the right. (Ah, so that's why.) Additional typical embroidery locations include the lower sleeve for polos and cuffs for long sleeve woven shirts. Note that cuff embroidery is facing upside down to the wearer so the customer can read it right side up. Other locations may be available, but it depends on the particular garment in question. Be aware, though, that embroidering in multiple or difficult locations can increase your cost dramatically.

8. Color of Embroidery. Usually you can have multiple color threads in the same logo for no additional charge. From the supplier we use, you can have up to 10 colors at no additional charge; your particular supplier's maximum color limit may vary. If you have a particular PMS (Pantone Matching System) color that needs to be matched, it can be done, but it may involve additional fees.

9. Size of Embroidery. For polos, woven shirts, and jackets, around a 3" x 3" embroidered left chest logo area is typically a maximum. For polo lower sleeve and woven shirt cuffs, usually 1" x 2" is maximum (sometimes smaller). Other embroidery location sizes vary. However, always check before creating any design for embroidery.

10. Artwork. Though embroidery can emulate shading, remember that each shade in your artwork is a different thread. With shading in your logo, you'll hit that 10 color thread color maximum in a hurry. Your logo artwork must be crisp, clean, non-gradient vector artwork to achieve the best embroidery possible. See a full discussion on artwork in the chapter titled *"What is Good Artwork for Imprinting?"*

CHAPTER 40:
4 Tips for Handling Rush Promotional Product Orders

Okay, a confession. Sometimes I'm the promotional products distributor who doesn't get promo ordered early for my next event. It's the old plumber with the leaky faucet scenario again. However, I usually can rectify the situation in a short period of time, and not because I'm in the promo business either. It's because I use these rush order handling tips:

1. Develop a List of Go-To Suppliers for Rush Projects. I have two absolutely awesome suppliers who can turn orders around for me and ship them out the next business day if I get my order in by a designated time. Establish relationships with dependable go-to sources that you can rely on when the pressure's on. Develop those relationships BEFORE you need them. Familiarize yourself with their product offerings so you know what your options are.

2. Have Your Production-Ready Artwork Ready to Go at All Times. Clean, vector artwork is an absolute necessity for promotional product imprinting. Make sure that you have your logo artwork in an .eps (Encapsulated

Postscript) or .ai (Adobe Illustrator) format available to forward to your promotional product vendor. This will avoid delays caused by having to do a redrawing of your logo which could take up to several days. If you won't be able to have a clean logo ready for a rush order, be prepared to go with a simple text imprint.

3. Have "Plan B" Choices. Even if you've developed relationships with your go-to suppliers and are pretty confident in their ability to have inventory available on a moment's notice, realize that there may be the occasion where stock may be low or out. Plan on making at least one or two additional "Plan B" product choices in case your "Plan A" choice fails.

4. Have Your Payment Scenario Planned. Many suppliers will ask for prepayment on rush orders, usually via credit card. So arrange in advance for a business credit card you will use for rush situations so you don't end up having to use your personal credit lines.

I know I'm not alone in this gotta-get-it-now scenario. In the past few years, we have processed more rush orders than at any time in our company's history.

CHAPTER 41:
Do Promotional Products Have a Shelf Life?

Usually, when you receive your promotional product order, you don't generally see an expiration date on your shipment. But, yes, it does have a shelf life.

So here's a recap of general guidelines for shelf life on some popular promotional products:

Food Items. Some food items may be marked with expiration dates, but not all are. Though mints, jelly beans, hard candy, pretzels, chocolates, beverages, etc. are typically considered non-perishable items, that does not mean they can be stored or safely consumed indefinitely and should usually be used within a few weeks to a couple of months at most. There are several food items, such as fresh baked cookies, that could have significantly shorter shelf life than other items, sometimes just a few days. Some products, such as chocolate or cheese, may require refrigerated transport and storage, especially in warmer weather. Check with your promotional products distributor for specific expiration dates and manufacturer safety, storage and handling recommendations when purchasing.

Pens. About 1 year, although some may last longer. After that point, inks begin to dry out and skipped writing starts to occur. (Trying to write with a dry pen just sets my teeth on edge!)

Personal Care. Lip balms, sunscreens, hand sanitizers, etc. may already come with expiration dates stamped on them. They may have limited shelf life. Observe any storage instructions and safety information printed on the products and ask your promotional products consultant if you have questions.

Paper Goods. Up to about 1 year for adhesive notes is a good guide, although some may last longer. The adhesive may begin to deteriorate over time. Non-adhesive paper items generally have quite a long shelf life if kept out of sunlight and in a cool, dry place.

Wearable Items. Could last years if stored in dry, cool conditions. Ink imprints should last, but could deteriorate if not stored with care.

Almost Everything Else. 1 year rule-of-thumb guideline since you'll be bored with your promotion by that time!

About Heidi Thorne

Dr. Heidi Thorne, MBA/DBA, is an author and business speaker who focuses on small business and marketing topics. She has over 25 years of experience in sales, advertising, marketing and public relations, including a decade in the hospitality and trade show industries. As well, she was a trade newspaper editor for over 15 years, has blogged since 2010 and taught at the college level for five years.

Books. Heidi has written several books and eBooks on business and self publishing. For a current listing of all books, with links to purchase, visit the "Books" page at HeidiThorne.com.

Speaking. Need a speaker for your business event? Let Heidi engage and entertain your audience! For video previews and current topics, visit the "Speaking" page at HeidiThorne.com.